THE MIND'S EYE

THE MIND'S EYE

Essays by

EDMUND BLUNDEN

Essay Index Reprint Series

BOOKS FOR LIBRARIES PRESS, INC.
FREEPORT, NEW YORK

First published 1934
Reprinted 1967

LIBRARY OF CONGRESS CATALOG CARD NUMBER:
67-28745

PRINTED IN THE UNITED STATES OF AMERICA

CONTENTS

7

CONTENTS

PART THREE
ENGLAND

PART FOUR
THE WORLD OF BOOKS

To

SYLVA

who does these things better

AUTHOR'S NOTE

MOST of these papers have been seen in print else-where, as contributions to periodicals here and as far away as Japan; one of them was published first in Messrs. Cobden-Sanderson's miscellany, *Little Innocents*. I hope, if I spare the reader the tedium of a detailed list, I shall not offend the editors who originally permitted these articles to appear, and mostly paid for them. There were many other essays of the sort which might have been recovered, but I believe the present selection represents them also; and, once mislaid, old newspapers and journals take a long time to recapture. In any case, indolence in this may prove to have been as good as a virtue

E. B.

PART ONE

FLANDERS

WAR AND PEACE

How mysterious that after so many years, not inactive, not undramatic, nor passed without much delight and discovery in man and nature, I find myself frequently living over again moments of experience on the Western Front. The war itself with its desperate drudgery is not the predominant part of these memories – I need a more intense word than memories; it is Nature as then disclosed by fits and starts, as then most luckily encountered 'in spite of sorrow,' that so occupies me still. The mind suddenly yields to simple visions. Pale light striking through clouds in shafts, like the sunrays of Rembrandt, beyond the mute and destined tower of Mesnil, continues inextinguishably to lure me. The ramping weeds in their homespun fringing the chalky road to grim Beaumont Hamel seem to be within my reach. The waterfowl in the Ancre pools and reed-beds exchange their clanking monosyllables with an aerial clearness, as though there were no others in the ten years between. I think to pick up the rosy-cheeked apples fallen in the deserted, leaf-dappled, grassy gunpits in the orchards of Hamel. And then some word from my companion calls me to lose no more time with our bomb-boxes on the menacing village road.

Perhaps these moments recur according to the season, for it is now autumn, and our share in the Somme fighting began towards the end of a splendid August. Looking back a little, to May and June, I see that this year I was chiefly haunted by seasonable recollections. Now it would be the moon on the white ghost of a house and the white-flowering bush before it in Festubert, with the noise of our ration wagons dying out along the road: now pale cherries, now buoyant apple-blossom brightened our restless camps a mile or two behind, with the guns at their hoarse work close by. Under a plank bridge carrying a trench tramway a nameless runnel whispered, with tiny fish revelling in their brief brilliant existence. Cars and lorries passed apace on the day's business below that twinkling, towering avenue of trees ranked northward out of Béthune – *species aeternitatis*. A sudden sighing came through the swampy sedge behind unholy Cuinchy, to me standing alone near the last dreary silent cottage, under a sky of freakish monster-clouds and rainy sunset. And if this winter is not contrary to the last, I shall often seem to be in Flanders, while the smoky gloom of dull weather gloats upon the dark unfruiting clay, the sweating house-walls, the sulky stained ditches; or the spectral snow-light of dawn will begin to define the long shutters over the broken windows of some punished white chateau, now untidily tenanted by genuine 'old soldiers' in charge of stores. Against a bitter blue the jag of St. Jean church-tower on the ridge will shiningly overtop the black spikes of trees while we stumble eastward on the glassy pavé; and then, swift relief! I am on Mont Kokereele in the hurling gusts of rain, while the driven, withering bramble claws here and there in the air over the quarry and finds no rest, and the streaming hazels wrestle, until on a sudden the day brightens and we who dig there cease to dig, with words of delight and wonder. For to the south-east a new transparency seems created; the vast plain 'sweeps with all its lessening towers' mile after mile, all calm, all distinct, villages and woods, towns and highways in the beauty of order; some of the gleaming churches mark our long past marchings, and beyond all, like monuments of our experience, we see the dominant Fosses of the black country towards Lens.

That brief phenomenon of magnified and purged sight, when the sun returned through the rain, may best explain what my words cannot – the transforming clarity of such reperceptions as I have exemplified. At such moments one's mortal franchise seems to be enlarged, and a new sphere of consciousness opened. I go a great distance in no time, and hear bells rung in secret. Why should the war leave such effects? God forgive me if they were the only remembrance of the Western Front still vivid to me; in fact they are the singular prologues to long and strenuous enactions of a drama beside which, even in partial and imperfect view, Mr. Hardy's *Dynasts* lacks profundity and appalment. They are the puzzling, unanticipated, and ever swiftly concealed side of the picture, and as such I note them, wondering whether ordinary life without the fierce electricity of an overwhelming tempest of forces and emotions could project such deep-lighted detail.

(1925)

AFTERTONES

THE summer of 1918 drifted past with its eddies of intrigue and dispute and rumour in the camp and the world beyond. It was a camp among ancestral trees, copses, meadows, cornfields bubbling with poppies, windmills on their little heights of goat-grazed turf; besides, the sky was blue and the air southern; yet I screen my eyes from that summer. The delight of being away from France after almost two years of ruins and ever-spreading terror was not itself wholly good; youth, now certain of a short time to live, through some magic dispensation of the War Office, did strange things in a world which it had never had the time to study. Moved by some instinct of spiritual pride, I no sooner arrived in the camp for my six months' respite than I wrote — I 'had the honour to submit' — my application to be allowed to return to France, where such unpleasant German manœuvres were proceeding. The application received no answer, except amused comment from an old major before dinner. I waited a week, then repeated my appeal with more eloquence. This time the Doctor was ordered to examine me; he said that I was unfit to return overseas. It was kind, and before many weeks in the camp it became true. But I was not finished yet. I had the blank half of the warrant which carried me from France, only cancelled in copying pencil. I considered the necessary innocent forgery, which offered no apparent difficulty. The only trouble would be in getting my valise (with books) to the station, eight miles off. However, I already knew a man with a pony-trap. It was merely a question of choosing the night for shooting the moon.

Then one morning I was ordered to assist at a court of inquiry in a town. This had the side-result of a romance, so immediate and complete as to seem love at first sight; my midnight stratagem and my warm fancy of surprising my old battalion in some trench or farm buildings behind Kemmel were set aside. Now began the real grimness of that shining summer in England. First of all, it was a bad camp. Next, there was almost always a stealthy hatred between those who had never 'been out', or had taken one joy ride behind the battlefield and an overseas-service chevron, and the returned B.E.F. man, who was presumed to be no 'soldier'. Then again, the place was merely a mill for the purpose of crushing the soul out of eighteen-year-old boys and sending them wholesale into the world's fiercest furnaces. And there were personal sources of misery. Overworked, insulted and ill, some of us broke out into tirades against our oppressors, and for a time paid heavily for our uncontrol. It might be amusing now to recall some of these moments; but not altogether; enough to note

how one of them became tragic. A sergeant-major —
a fighting man — was 'broken' on some ground or
other which seemed unimportant. On church parade
he talked to me of the case, but did not mention his
plan; the next I heard was that he had committed
suicide, leaving letters to say that he hoped his action
might be for the good of his survivors in the camp. A
mutiny followed. After the restoration of 'law and
order', I one day took a draft of two hundred 'eighteen-
year-olds' to the troop train, and was going round the
sections, wishing I was going farther with them, when
the colonel appeared. It was embarrassing. There
were groans and booings all along the train.

But I delay. When my orders for France at last
arrived, I was in bed, struggling with asthma. The
attempt to obey the orders landed me in hospital,
under considerable distress; and, when I emerged, I
was sent on to another camp, still ill. Days of pale,
damp autumn brought November 11th, and the
hooting of sirens in the harbour below the parade
ground on which we were engaged as usual. Nobody
had expected an armistice, and nobody was excited by
it. All assembled round the orderly room, wishing
that the colonel would celebrate the event with a
speech; but he avoided the historic opportunity. Two
or three days later I was ordered to France, and this
time I had no trouble in arriving there except the
task of shepherding several hundred scarcely happy
men of all regiments into their base-camp.

Such journeys were too monotonous to be remembered. The usual scramble to the engine for
hot water, and the usual rapid hunt for coke and wood
round any cabins beside the line, took place at the
halts. I looked out for Tincques, which had curiously
remained in my memory from the time when we were
passing on our way to the old Somme battle. We
detrained at Douai, and I immediately felt the once-
imagined, singular excitement in moving freely where
the German soldier had been billeted. It was too late;
but what would not one have given in 1916 to be an
invisible man for a day or two and see how brother
Boche was enjoying life? The city was not entirely
without suggestion of its dignified history, but the
dirtiness of retreat had yet to be cleansed. It had been
on the edge of destruction, and was now merely a
clearing-house for troops and traffic. The smell of old
blankets, wet boots and wood-smoke came from the
dark holes of the barracks in the November twilight.
Leaving the men there with whom I was joining a
battalion still farther on towards Germany, I took my
doubtful way along the canal, examining shell-holes
and the litter of machine-gun posts that once – not
many hours ago – made that canal devilish. I saw an
empty building strewn with papers; taking one, I read
a German advertisement for condensed milk. But the
packing-cases all round were torn open and contained
no sample. Douai was like that. By a conservatory
door I found what looked like a book of essays in good

binding. But there was no text. The whole place was the book of life without the inside.

Marching on from this husk of masonry next day, we crossed a plain of coaldust tracks and grey grass, of church spires and chimneys; this trampled country continued for miles, but presently the villages and lands wore a better freshness. Here and there a lonely house on a causeway had been unlucky in the final fighting. One such exposed its deadness at the approach to Hornaing, where I joined my new battalion. The process is always a little unnerving, and to me, with the sense that I ought to have been in France all 1918, it was more than so. However, there were the landmarks plain enough: battalion head-quarters and mess, company headquarters, the canteen, the regimental sergeant-major, and one's billet. The white and red houses were all much alike; from some of them emerged girls much older than their years, and old men who lived without apparent nourishment. Some of the women of the place were not very well pleased with the peace; generally, yes, but personally, no. I guessed at the circumstances of these strained apprehensive faces. Leaving company head-quarters in the first evenings, I could feel much the same difficulty in the abrupt change from a long war to silence. I scanned the eastern darkness as though, if I looked hard enough, the familiar line of lights would be playing there. The silent darkness was in some way worse than those assistants of vengeance. I wanted them. Youth had been subdued to what it worked in.

The old officers of the battalion, who had seen it through, proved to be restless and irritable. They saw disintegration advancing. The men, seeing no special necessity for kicking their heels in a nondescript French village without my 'line of lights', went about their routine without enthusiasm. Drill, marching, inspections, games, concert parties and educational intentions filled in the time. The best diversion was salvaging in woods and marshes and windy beetfields, but we found little; and my one pair of boots was not equal to these occasions. I was never in a worse billet: the floor was of mud and the enormous mattress was damp beyond help. Rations and supplies altogether became meagre. They had to be brought by rail across the desolation between Arras and ourselves; and now discipline all over Europe was falling to dust, the old battlefield was haunted by looters, military and civilian. Still, the men clubbed together to get what vegetables the village could sell as a supplement to their meals; and the young women whose estaminet one knew would refer with pity to the far worse condition of even the German officers' table a few weeks earlier. 'Soup – our dog refused it.' There was a hope for the future if one considered this kind of remark, and the tenderness in it; but I was glad I was not one of those girls.

In an atmosphere, then, of discontent and indirection, we waited for 1919. Sometimes there was a lively evening, but it depended on make-believe rather than reality. Christmas duly produces a special celebration. It happened, however, that nothing to the purpose could be bought in our district, and with an officer named Browning (not unlike the poet in appearance) and two quartermaster-sergeants, I was sent off in good time to buy the Christmas dinner at Arras. When nowadays I think of buying my own dinner, I am surprised that 'out of all this great big world they'd chosen me' to strike a bargain with a Frenchwoman for a pig, cases of wine, hogsheads of beer, and other provisions. But so it was, and I was happy, for the train to Arras, swinging round Douai's red and grey mass across moist green and glittering water-lights, entered the former field of battle in daylight. 'Water, water every where', or rather ooze and slush, was working along old cuttings and trenches and holes of the yellow waste. The railway carried over such a swamp was a miracle. It was only just a railway. One could guess at the dead still lying about beyond the banks, even if the choked dugouts beside the rails were not full of them. Brown mounds of bricks with claws of machinery projecting, and a few huts with their round iron roofs, were all that rose from the famous plain. Roeux Chemical Works might have been any of these low heaps of waste. As we approached Arras, however, the valley of the Scarpe retained a pleasant ghost or two of the leafy past, and

25

lines of slender tree-shapes marked that last pathetic area of no-man's-land and British stand-to billets during the years of steady trenches.

Finding my way into a draughty house in Arras, used as a club, I signed the book – and above my signature I saw 'G. H. Harrison'. It was almost two years since I had seen my true colonel. I looked again: he had been here the day before. But perhaps he was staying? It was in vain; he had gone. I waited about, pretending to read, in case he should be coming back; but he did not, and a great and sudden hope went to the ground. Reduced afresh to the drifting mood of those days, I prowled in Arras and saw the landmarks, the still towering Hotel de Ville and the square with its grey house-fronts ('Spanish Square'), its enlarged cellars still looking like man's real home, its barbed-wire barricades. On the whole the German gunners had treated Arras kindly; but at its eastern bounds the nakedness of the land began instantly. At present it was still a 'downstairs' town. The vast rooms aloft would not be easy to return to. I found a shop open, chiefly selling soap and sardines, in the ground floor of a fine house, with a flag over the street; but overhead was vacancy and wreck.

Next day in a cold drizzle we walked out to a village called Dainville, and inquiring at an estaminet controlled by two sisters who had not seen four years of the British soldier for nothing, found that our Christmas dinner could be supplied. It would cost more than usual – but we had to have it. One more night in Arras, with old trench-maps and the *Life of Keats* for company – then back to Dainville, and concluding the deal. Foully cold as I was, I rejoiced in all this; there stood a fine farm with stone outhouses – should have been our billet; there, among half-lowered walls, a good corner for C company cookers; there, a pretty turning, the very thing for marching in by after a day in the practice trenches. Everything almost was fair or ugly, good or bad, according to its associations with the spirit of the B.E.F. But not everything: there was the citadel on our way into Arras – as at Ypres there had been some traces of hornwork and escarpment – to divert the feelings with the mysterious antiquity of British expeditions to these simple places.

The slate-tinted reflection of watery paving and creeping ditches dies away into cold darkness with a wind from the east, from those places which I never knew and which I now conjecture to be more savage and hopeless than any I did know: Gavrelle, and Wancourt, and Roeux. I am in a mental blind alley. This is Arras, full of the domestic echoes of our army, our armies; I was ever an antiquary, and searched the hummocks of Ypres like an Orientalist in Xanadu; I should be going about Arras and reading every syllable of her ancient and modern drama, the comic reliefs and the tragic impacts alike. But again, I am out of tune. It needs the old faces, voices, songs, jests, Colonel Harrison, the sequence and limitation of

27

trench warfare. Meanwhile, the metal of the gaping roof of Arras Station is the wind's dreary harmonium clanking and twanging; the swell of the wind comes flooding through the cold platforms with a mockery of the past or the future habits of railways. From these feelings the arrival of the 'Christmas dinner' on a peasant's cart arouses me; we set about discovering whether there ever will be a train, other than the wind's creation, passing east through Arras, and, if there will, how to put our grimy cargo aboard from its place in the mud.

Midnight, more false rumours through the station, and at last an enormous train; we run our barrels and shoulder our boxes into the already overcrowded trucks of snoring or restless soldiers, tripping over heaps of equipment, and breathing the vapour of mud, sweat, greased leather, trodden food-scraps, and dirty water. It is a troop-train resembling rather that of some Balkan war than the not altogether unkempt horse-trucks of our old times in Flanders. A sapper who resented our forcing our goods into the gangway swears at and about us, with dark mouth and insane eye. We hope to be carried in this large coffin to the station nearest our battalion, but are not. A longer stop than usual brings us out on the track, questioning, receiving no replies, false replies; then at last a Frenchman tells us the train goes no farther. We watch him depart with his lantern; we believe he is right, and we unload our belongings. Later, we discover with no mean cunning that some trucks in an archway will go where we wish; the cold and slimy business of getting the 'Christmas dinner' along and forcing it all into the truck high above the track is repeated. The wind is still in the east. The clay-coloured daylight comes.

We arrive! I direct my companions to hurry up the four or five miles of cobbles to the battalion, and send transport; meanwhile I volunteer to watch the stacked cases and casks, which I have paid for on the battalion's account. Black-handed, black-jowled, black-streaked from head to foot, I wait; and an officer of military police comes for me, swinging a heavy revolver in his hand. 'Your papers.' The revolver is not swinging now. I put my dead fingers into my inner pocket, and hand him all I have – letters, officer's blue record-book, and what the hell's the matter with you? He with an anxious eye runs over the miscellany; hands part back; saunters with a careful ease into the station, returns and restores my blue book. 'All right. But I was looking for an Australian. Your stuff, I suppose? Ah, the battalion's Christmas dinner.' He retires into his office out of the wind; and I wait. No transport arrives. I am being prepared for influenza, but at last I decide against the process, and I give a call at the guard-room, where a sentry stands over some of His Majesty's property. A present, and a promise, seem to assure me, according to old traditions of this war, that my cases and casks

29

will be looked after by the sentries until I can see why the transport is not on the way; and I depart in relief, with aching eyes and shapeless feet. Unhappily for me, 'this war' ended in November. The transport, some hours later, receives our Christmas luxuries from the guard, but not all – the *blanc* is heavily lightened. I do not gain in reputation on this adventure; I take some days to recover my normal ill-health; and I am twenty pounds out of pocket.

Christmas, nevertheless, arrived and was celebrated; after this the chief purpose of our loitering in France appeared to be celebrating. The old German mess, with its curved and pointed ceilings, was a scene of many endeavours to rebel against the lethargy of armistice. Order went to the ropes more than once; there was a snowy disgraceful midnight when a venerable feud ended in a raid on the adjutant's billet. In his pyjamas this once Wolseyan youth was hauled into the road and soused in the icy slush. Why, only the instigator knew; but sympathetic assistants were not lacking after repeated draughts of apothecary's wine. Some afternoons we went off by any lorry that passed to Valenciennes or Denain; these excursions showed us little but successions of mine-craters at cross-roads, wood bridges outflanking the ruins of old and solid ones, and then greasy defaced streets with the wonderful German system of direction-boards conspicuous on houses and corners, and shop-windows coldly crying famine, and mad prices for soap and butter and bread.

Duty discovered some varieties for us. Working through the marshy plantations towards St. Amand, if we found little but an occasional belt of machine-gun cartridges or a revolver holster (one carried these trophies in with astonishment at the trouble, remembering the prodigious quantity of oddments wasted in and below the Somme battlefield) – wood-ranging here, I say, we had the relics of country beauty about us, and woolly-headed rushes whitened against the blue sky. An airplane plunged into a swamp; out we went with ropes and shovels, like the Lilliputians after Gulliver, and pushed and hauled and squashed and bawled. At night in my damp stable I read Elia and Verlaine, and sometimes my old host, a miner, would look in: 'Monsieur, je viens pour demander . . . une voiture pour aller aux mines . . . 'y-a du charbon là-bas. . . .' 'C'est que ma fille est malade . . . sans doute vous autres officiers vous avez des fruits sur la table, des oranges – elle désire surtout des oranges.' His son had managed to retain a lean yellow-rimmed bicycle, and went off on it frequently in the direction of the mines. But not for coal. Presently, after a donation of oranges, Mademoiselle recovered, and when I changed my billet in order to obtain a dry room for myself and my Charles Lamb, she came to see the lady of the house, and called on me with that pale face and grey-eyed mysteriousness – she warned me with strange emphasis against one or two of the girls of the parish. A queer world, this world of concealed meanings and magnetic accidents of human desire; how many are the voices that whisper, and could only be answered with years and years of event!

I do not know how my young indolent friend succeeded in keeping his spidery bicycle intact along the terrible roads by the slag-heaps, with the smoke creeping from them. The cobble-stones had been bulged by iron wheels into endless ups and downs, slippery with bad weather. Ordered one day to make a reconnaissance in and about the little town of Bouchain, we rode the usual ironclad army bicycles jarringly along the stumbling-blocks, and it happened that columns of lorries were passing us, sweeping the width almost of the way. We went ahead. Yet none of us was offered music-hall engagements. Bouchain was still Marlborough's town, or the Prince Eugène's. Its waterways defended it on the ancient principle. It slept. And yet it contained large modern barracks and horse-lines; its mill had been turned into a strong tower, where we climbed among the littered explosives, ever curious in our boredom. Along the river was a yard where the carcases of animals had been collected for the service of the German army; many of these carcases were still falling to pieces and mouldering down the banks into the poisoned stream. Vast and brilliant organization had dug out hidden acres of ammunition dumps in this area, and supplied underground trolleys on their rails, and systems of electricity;

these were dead, but the town of Bouchain only slept, and budded trees around the dilapidated houses awaited the spring.

Then came the chance for us. To Germany! and in a couple of days. I went to secure my rights of action once more. Then came a letter from home, with bad news, and urgently recalling me; and almost at once a call to the orderly-room followed. Some time before, our qualifications for being demobilized had been noted down, and I as a 'student' had the chance of being emancipated early. The major gave me the order for my departure. I thought of Germany, but the dark message I had had overwhelmed that speculation. I thanked him, and made up my mind. In any event, the period of dreary futility seemed about to end. No more of those 'lessons' from the French interpreter to fill in the evenings; no more blank stares over flat and watery plains. The question now was, what sort of train converted, or began to convert, the soldier into the civilian? Fancy was abroad, and she painted a luxury of travel – talked of cushioned and warmed compartments and a train-ferry to Richborough (it sounded to some ears like Richebourg). The actual journey was so great an ordeal that I wondered if we should see England. Winter returned with fangs; the cattle-truck was without even a brazier, and the wood-fire which I helped to keep going threatened to suffocate us or ignite the whole truck into a moving pyre. Two of the inmates lay under a blanket, ill. They had the new influenza. They died soon after they were 'detrained' on the long bleak siding at the base. I had seen war's ironies when we were in a manner equal to them, but these supplementary strokes were surely out of all bounds. Looking back over 1918 and this opening quarter of 1919, I became desperately confused over war and peace. Clearly, no man who knew and felt could wish for a second that the war should have lasted a second longer. But, where it was not, and where the traditions and government which it had called into being had ceased to be, we who had been brought up to it were lost men. Strangers surrounded me. No tried values existed now. I looked through the gashed linen window of the hut in the waiting-camp at the way down to the boat, deep in snow; I saw the unmanned cookhouses and 'ablution sheds'; and the sunnier hours of my old companionship at Béthune, and even in the valley of the Ancre, with their attendant loyalties and acceptances, seemed like sweet reason and lost love. Marching down to the docks, at the side of a great column of weary soldiers of all sorts, I was suddenly pulled up by an officer of about my own age, who, in a trembling voice demanded that I should at once improve the march discipline of the multitude, none of whom I had ever seen before. The Base Commandant, he warned me, would be on the look-out as we passed his headquarters. The Base Commandant had given orders that the marching of the troops should be maintained at the highest standard. 'Keep in your fours!', 'pick up the step there!' — but I did not succeed in reviving the martial spirit in those pestered, loaded, scrambling ranks with my thin reminders of a fantastic chivalry.

(1929)

THE SOMME STILL FLOWS

IT was a sunny morning, that of July 1st, 1916. The right notes for it would have been the singing of blackbirds and the ringing of the blacksmith's anvil. But, as the world soon knew, the music of that sunny morning was the guns. They had never spoken before with so huge a voice. Their sound crossed the sea. In Southdown villages the school-children sat wondering at that incessant drumming and the rattling of the windows. That night an even greater anxiety than usual forbade wives and mothers to sleep. The Battle of the Somme had begun.

This battle on the southern part of the British line overshadowed everything else. Even Ypres fell quiet. The three nations most prominently concerned on the Western Front concentrated their force in the once serene farmlands of Picardy. Their armies had arrived at a wonderful pitch of physical and spiritual strength. They were great organizations of athletes, willing to attempt any test that might be ordered. If the men of the Somme were probably unrivalled by any earlier armies, the materials and preparations of the battle were not less extraordinary. Railways, roads, motor transport, mules, water supply, aircraft, guns, mortars, wire, grenades, timber, rations, camps, telegraphic systems — all multiplied as in some absurd vision.

Many of you who are reading now still feel the fever of that gathering typhoon.

Such monstrous accumulations, and transformations of a countryside which in the sleepier period of its war had been called 'The Garden of Eden', could not be concealed from the intended victims. Surprise on the large scale was impossible. But the British devised local surprises; rapidly dug jumping-off positions; field guns waiting to fire from the front trenches; the terrific mine ready to go up at La Boisselle. The defenders also had their secrets prepared for July 1st.

At last the moment came for mutual revelations. Villages, wiped out in a few hours, earned reputations for hopeless horror when our men rose in the daylight from their already destroyed positions and moved to capture them. Some of them they did capture. Few who survived long enough under German guns and machine-guns to enter the trenches opposite could have retained any illusions. They found themselves in a great trap of tunnels and concrete and steel rails and iron entanglements. From holes in the land they had crossed, from higher ground north and south, from untouched gunpits, these isolated men were also wiped out. I knew a colonel whose hair turned white in this experience. I knew Thiepval, in which battalions disappeared that day. I knew Thiepval Wood, before which in the mud of November were withering bodies of the British and German combatants of July 1st.

The outbreak of the Somme battle may be described as a tremendous question-mark. By the end of the day both sides had seen, in a sad scrawl of broken earth and murdered men, the answer to that question. No road. No thoroughfare. Neither race had won, nor could win, the War. The War had won, and would go on winning. But, after all the preparation, the ambition, the ideals and the rhythms of these contending armies, there could not be any stopping. To-morrow is always another day, and hope springs eternal. The battle of the Somme would continue from summer to winter. The experiment of the century must be repeated, varied, newly equipped. Perhaps luck would play a part. Perhaps external conditions would affect these machine-gun emplacements, and the lucky lads from Adelaide or Sunderland walking onward through the explosions.

Accordingly, what had been begun on July 1st became a slow slaughtering process; the Somme might have been a fatal quicksand into which division after division was drawn down. In order to illustrate that remark, I am going to sketch the history of the division in which I served during the offensive. Though we were far north of the battlefield in June, 1916, we nevertheless came under its fiery influence; for, on the last day of June, we were sent into a 'minor operation' as they called it, with the object of keeping back German troops and artillery from the real affair. Our brigade assaulted; crossed a flat water-meadow, full of deep dykes and thick barbed wire, under every kind of fire; and a great many of us were dead or wounded within a couple of hours. 'Like a butcher's shop', said a plain-spoken private to the general next day. When we had to some extent recovered from this minor operation, the powerful and ominous words came round, 'We're going South'.

War is not all war, and there lies the heart of the monster. 'Going South' was at first more like a holiday adventure than the descent to the valley of the shadow. I still make myself pictures of that march, and could not guess at any summer days more enchanting. The very fact that, after ceaseless rumours and contradictions, we were now certainly destined for the Somme battle made us shut our minds to the future and embrace the present. We marched with liberal halts through wooded uplands, under arcades of elms, past mill-streams and red and white farms; and, as we marched, we sang. Not even the indifferent map-reading of the boyish officer at the head of the battalion could damp our spirits. What were kilo-metres? At twilight we took over our billets in clay-walled barns, or farmhouses with vineleaves at the windows and 'café, monsieur' at any moment. Every man knew his neighbour. Never was such candour or such confidence.

We stayed longer at the hamlet which provided our training-ground. Indeed, its chalky hillsides were said to be precisely similar to our future share of the

Somme battlefield. In an interval of our successful attacks on the dummy trenches of our ghostly enemy, we lay down by companies while some particularly well-nourished experts from General Headquarters eulogized the beauty of the bayonet. We went to sleep. Presently rainy weather set in, but when we continued our journey to the battle the sun burned and the dust rose along the road. It was towards the end of August.

After several postponements we made our first appearance in the fighting. We did not know, most of us, that the lines which we had dreams of capturing had been attacked on July 1st. But, as I stared across a valley at the German positions, a day or two before our action, I was puzzled by a small heap of what was clearly British barbed wire, on its original reels, a long way behind the enemy's front trench. In the cold early mist of September 3rd our division went over. A few astonishing officers and men fought their way to those coils of wire. One or two returned from them in the evening, by which time history had repeated itself. The shattered battalions withdrew from the valleys and ridges still echoing with bombardment and the pounding of machine guns. The Somme had pulled us under once, and we emerged just gasping. Somewhere to the south there had been a success.

We did not withdraw far. We quickly returned to the line and remained in the trenches, from which two mighty attacks had been launched, week upon week.

South, there was still a vague hope. Trenches were said to be changing hands beyond Thiepval Hill, which still frowned upon our ragged remains of trenches. We witnessed and heard furious attacks in that direction, rolling smoke, bursts of flame, soaring signal-lights; but these closed in autumn darkness. One day a sensation was caused. Down there in the south the British had made an attack with Tanks, which we understood to be as big as houses and capable of pushing houses down. Then the Somme was still a promising experiment!

For our own next attack we had no assistance of tanks. It was now a long age since July 1st and its blue skies. Yet October 21st was a still, frosty day. A surprise was reserved for our opponents: we were to attack a few minutes after noon. We did. Some of us had now seen three attacks, others had just arrived from the barrack-squares, where sacks of straw are nimbly transfixed by unshelled and unbombed soldiers. We took our trench, and were then submitted to artillery concentration, which went on two days. There were enough of us left to hand over the conquered ground to the 'next for the barber', and to crawl back through endless shell-holes and dead. The captured trench was partly floored with bodies.

Almost at once we were in the line again, and after some days of curious peace we moved to a desperate mud-field east of Thiepval – one of the classic terrors

of the Western Front. The year was breaking up now.
The craters were swimming with foul water. What was
left of the trenches became lanes of yellow and blood-
brown slime, deeper than our average height. The
tracks beside them were usually smoking with accurate
gunfire. The alternative was, generally, to be blown
to pieces or to be drowned. After several days of the
Schwaben Redoubt, with the corpses choking the
dugout entrances, we were informed of another
surprise arranged for the enemy. Our division was to
take part in a large attack. This occurred on
November 13th. The division surpassed itself, capturing ground and one labyrinth of dugouts with many
hundreds of Germans in them. Still, there was no
sign yet of the fabled green country beyond the Somme
battle. That evening I was sent forward with a runner
on a reconnaissance. It was growing dark, a drizzling
rain was steadily increasing, and on every side was the
glare and wailing and crashing of bombardment.
We passed through the new posts of the British
advance, shivering in water-holes, and then we went
blindly astray. After our painful wandering through
the barrages of two artilleries and the crazy ruins of
trench and battery systems, we were lucky enough to
find a way back. That night, retracing our adventure
with the colonel and his maps, we found that we had
been in the outskirts of a village named Grandcourt.
Grandcourt! We felt a little proud. But it came out
that some British soldiers had made their miraculous

way to that village through the German forts and fire on that remote summer's morning, July 1st.

After this winter battle we left the Somme — but who were 'we'? Not those who had marched south in the time of ripening orchards; a very different body of men. We had been passed through the furnace and the quicksand. What had happened to this division was typical of the experience of all divisions, in all the armies. There is no escape from the answer given on July 1st to the question of the human race. War had been 'found out', overwhelmingly found out. War is an ancient impostor, but none of his masks and smiles and gallant trumpets can any longer delude us; he leads the way through the cornfields to the cemetery of all that is best. The best is, indeed, his special prey. What men did in the battle of the Somme, day after day, and month after month, will never be excelled in honour, unselfishness, and love; except by those who come after and resolve that their experience shall never again fall to the lot of human beings.

(1929)

WE WENT TO YPRES

I LOOKED south-east out of the bedroom window, which was lofty, but approachable by means of a kind of fire-step. Those were the hills that knew so much. That would be Verbrandenmolen, with a new wind-mill. From the railway cutting past Hill Sixty, puffs of steam rose in white clouds and thinned away. It was a suspicious appearance, in that particular spot — but it really meant nothing unkind. Southward, Mount Kemmel was green almost as in the days before the bonfire of 1918, and I thought I could make out the toy observatory among the trees. Summer's evening light was over all the place; not casting its splendours, but, as I would have had it, veiled in soft rainy warmth.

Nearer, below, was the railway station of Ypres, a humble structure which no one would have mistaken for a town hall. I had never stepped from a train there until this evening. Indeed I had only seen two or three ration-trains in this city; they used to occur, without lights, beside an old timber-dump on the west side. They amazed us, first by arriving, and then by getting away. But here was the correct, authorized, official station doing its duty. Nothing strange, of course, to see young clerks, schoolgirls, soldiers on furlough, market-dames emerging past a ticket-collector into a cobbled Place. But I found it a little strange.

Just round the corner I looked for company head-quarters. The last time I turned that corner, a shell had killed two men beneath the shining shell-cases hung as gas-gongs. I could not now discover which was the house above the still distinctly-remembered basement, any more than which was the house with the painted swans on its shrapnel-spattered inner walls, or that which supplied me with a few books as I balanced along the unfallen beams of the upper storey. But things like that must be. At least I was geographically 'about right'. The Ramparts were not so baffling. Lovers sat on the benches above them, and below, and a pike made a dash among the lilies; but I knew the curves and inlets of the moat, and remembered the setting of the churches, St. Pierre and St. Jacques, between the Lille and the Menin Gate. Of our former shelters, most traces were gone. The stylish canvas latrine, for instance, which was specially reserved for the 'G.O.C., ——th Inf. Bde', no longer stood like a lodge at the entrance to our estate — the brick vault traversing the Ramparts. But that vault was there, with a doorway (padlocked). Looking in, I saw that the far end (on which German telescopes once were pointed) had been opened, to afford a passage to an allotment on the edge of the moat.

But older soldiers might have found still more of their Ramparts. My walks along the top had almost all been in the flame-tormented dark, and now, without embarrassing the ardent couples in their tenancy, I could see by the quiet light an unsuspected staircase of Vauban's, leading down to a dugout that will probably be there if ever it is wanted again. The Lille Gate no longer gave me prospect of a smoke and drink downstairs with the 'Electric Light Company', but its internal architecture, perhaps even older than Vauban, seemed to be in existence. Where were our swans that haunted these recesses? The new Menin Gate hardly seemed to have the perpetuity of the Ramparts each side. Its marble was not 'to the manner born'. Raising my eyes to the names of those who knew it well, the first I could read was that of my friend C., and I grudged that and the other names. The Ramparts did not seem to want them. How intensely we want them!

Another day; it is the weather in which Waterloo was fought, and the scene is similar, I imagine, with all its peasant property, its velvet-green, its tethered red-sided heifers, its muddy pavements outside drab beer-houses at cross-roads. Everything, except the tag ends of villages and the track, seems richer by the harrowing of war. It is ridiculous to be depressed by the triumph of life, but I feel a little grey as I move in this vernal world, marvellously re-flourishing. I am grateful to the low drumfire of the thunder, and the sudden, cold, slashing, thorough rainstorm which makes us crouch under an outhouse wall in Zillebeke, a stone's throw from the church. But this moment of contact is ended by an enterprising taxi-driver, who has had word of visitors *walking* in Zillebeke. He pulls up to propose the advantages of his vehicle, and the good sense of employing him to show us Mount Sorrel, Hill Sixty, and a series of other names. Feebly we assent. After all, the war is over, infinitely over, and we are half-drowned and (who would have forseen it?) weary of a couple of miles of stone road. We know by now what he means by Hill Sixty. It will be a souvenir shop, a window displaying several brands of beer, a slippery patch of ground enclosed by wire fences, and a placarded hole or two like the rubbish-dumps of any village, but without so much iron.

This view proved to be correct enough. But before leaving Ypres, we had resourcefully noticed an advertisement of Original Fire Trenches in this neighbourhood. I mentioned that to our driver. He was prepared for it. He was going there. The taxi drew up near a hovel or two, with directions to the trenches; but before one could set eyes on those memorials, a small fee was payable. It was received by a 'character', a tall, wild, voluble young man like a backwoodsman, with a remarkable command of English. He at once began speaking enthusiastically of the discovering of remains of all sorts, especially

47

bodies. He complained (in such a way as said 'However, we live') that it was far from Ypres, and so the ten francs allowed by the authorities for the bringing home of a British soldier was not easy money. 'The German Government,' he said, 'don't pay us anything, so we don't trouble to report the German bodies we find'. He expected approval, but one of us was a German, and I said, 'But these German soldiers were fine men, and. . . .' 'Oh yes, sir,' he rapidly interrupted, catching the idea, 'yes, very fine soldiers. Now these are the trenches, and I am to-day opening another communication trench'. A small boy with a shovel, at these words, began scooping out a little mud and water from the winding ditch. 'You see this boot? Those are the original toes in it. There, look, that's the original galvanized iron.' 'What's this trench called?' 'Warrington C.T.,' he guessed. I had been in these trenches before, and had been paid for it! 'That's a bit of an ammunition box. . . .' The small boy again like an automaton flung out his shovelful, but drew a blank.

The least transformed war-ground at Ypres, last summer, was that along the canals, both that from the Lys, and the Yser Canal. Not that the lineaments of war were obvious. But there was not yet a racial reconquest. The birds and frogs in the reeds were unmolested, the waterway was doing nothing but lie in the sun and rain; nothing of our old shelters stood along the banks, but you could find a wrenched and pierced length of roofing in the soft soil where, here and there, it showed the ancient arrival of a shell. We found a shell even. Along those banks, probably half a million shells came down. Trespassing away, we found some wooden posts along the little Yperlee, once part of dugouts in which generals discussed Z Day; and here was a concreted doorway, leading nowhere. I pushed it, and a slab of concrete promptly tumbled into the Yperlee. Farther along, there was more concrete — the medical dugouts at Essex Farm. These by all the laws should have ceased to exist twelve years earlier. They stood then in a very 'windy corner', and as I passed them, though not pausing to reflect, I thought that they would soon be struck by something larger than usual. No — here they were in a warm day of blue skies and flowery breezes, themselves dark and dank. But you could lean against them, and they did not fall. I hope they have not fallen. At least, if they have done, they had an uncommon lease of life in the days when Flanders was ejecting Britain and Germany before her army of small-holders, and preparing the Grand Place of Ypres for new wars of liberty. The walls blazoned forth the doings of a swollen Red Giant, who was booting a top-hatted bourgeois in black, clean out of the immortal Salient.

(1930)

THE EXTRA TURN

G., IN a moment of weary activity, has repaired the primitive neglected gramophone which, I remember, he resolutely carried home and demobilized from the Western Front. It is precisely similar to one which was a friend of ours in 1916, on the edges of that battle of the Somme which was so unfavourable to gramophones and their owners. As soon as he produced the specimen from his perpetual salvage dump, I knew that there would be trouble; and when he had succeeded in making it rehearse a few pieces — Beethoven's 'Minuet', the 'Largo', Pierné's 'Serenade' seemed inevitably to come forward — the trouble was in full flood. But G., who has no real passion for antiquity, then compelled his machine to be comparatively modern, and we heard the loud, hot, joyful lyric of the 'King's Horses, and Men' —

They're not out to fight the foe,
You might think so, but O dear no!
They're here because they've got to go
To put a little pep into the Lord Mayor's Show.

I left them at it; I had been called to a distance where

the King's Men, it seemed, were still engaged in shows of another sort.

You see the trouble. One does one's best to live with the date, but accidents happen. Happy are those who on January 1st, 1932, are able to belong to January 1st, 1932. Perhaps I must surrender. I hate this large calendar here. The spirit in which it and a dozen others were given to me was exquisite. I could picture L. at the stationer's, trying to select the One that — subject to little preferences of L., I mean — would suit my taste, eyesight, study-table, and forgetfulness. But what is the use to me of this vast red warning? No wonder if I have not torn off the leaves for a fortnight. The numbers on them vary — I admit it; but they are all one.

For, if it had not been the gramophone, the baffling of my sense of time present would have arrived in another form. It was lucky for me that, when I shared the 'Standing Room Only' the other evening, Mr. George Robey had changed his stage character so boldly from that of years ago, and was principally a 'German musical phenomenon' (and some of them guffawed when this expert confessed 'he could not spick English so well what he could before der War!'). Had Mr. Robey been resuscitating the songs from *The Bing Boys*. . . . But, I think, my luck was fair that evening. How immensely hard our gramophone worked in 1916, obedient to the commands of *The Bing Boys*! How maliciously and gaily did our colonel, who had some doubts as to the efficiency, in the matter in hand, of Liberal leaders, recite and variegate that stanza:

In Parliament to-day when they get into a stew,
When they're all mixed up, and they don't know what
  to do,
Mr. Asquith says, in a voice *serene* and *calm*,
'Another little drink wouldn't do us any harm'.

The same colonel — time and the Bavarians over the way permitting — would listen to the 'Largo', and assert presently that for him there was one of the outstanding and permanent things in the shaken world.

But I have not yet told you where and when our gramophone was at its best. You may not know the Somme battlefield (beetfield now, I trust, and orchards even). Somewhere out to the east of Amiens there was a village called Beaumont Hamel, on a broad chalk hill that descended to a once romantic millstream, the Ancre. Beaumont Hamel being in its last days a fortress, and indeed Germany's masterpiece of brain-work, spadework and ironwork, we were restricted to trenches a little apart from its western tree-stumps. And beautiful trenches too, but for an ugly corner or two; and over them the September sun burned, and a young line of aspens silvered with musical restlessness at their western entry. And over them the guns made argument, and into them the fires descended. The season-change of apple boughs and berried hedgerows tapestried the sky behind us, where we lived in a kind of log-cabin and white house in one, annexed to the trench called Second Avenue. Northward we saw the grey structures of another local headquarters position, White City, and the lower bricks and windows of a sugar refinery. Southward, we cared not to look too often. It was not the slanted crucifix above the tombs of *cultivateurs* there, or the displaced marbles and wreaths, that caused this peculiarity in us. It was the battle of the Somme, in which we had lately been plunged very powerfully — a mile south, two miles; a couple of hours down the road and round and up again where roads ended.

Meanwhile, Beaumont Hamel was reasonably tolerant of us. There might be an outburst now and then, but much might be said on both sides. On our territory, just above the old Beaumont Road (which in those days might have proposed to the tourist with just as much credit an access to Saturn), a cave existed under a hillock, with a crevice in the roof, through which a heavy trench-mortar shot up its Flying Pigs. These tinned projectiles, even when they collide with nobody in particular, have all the elements of un-popularity about them. The unpopularity extends even to those who handle them. F., how often have I regarded you, with all your blameless life and religious inheritance, as not a fit companion for youth! It was Sidneian virtue in our colonel to invite even F. into the log cabin for a drink and a tune.

Often — we stayed weeks in those trenches — the evening came on nearly as still as in Milton's vision, and guests arrived for dinner and the gramophone; while the green starlight gleamed, and greener pearl-chains of tracer shells went up from somewhere at something in the air. Pratt the gunner, with his indiscretions from Brock's Benefit and its explosive neighbourhood, was the favourite visitor. I do not know quite why I am telling my reader these things; Pratt is dead and gone, and after all, we hardly knew him ourselves in point of — the Calendar. We only held those trenches a month. But, I conjecture, there is a reason; on shipboard, they say, people soon fall in love; in war, you fall in friendship, and know your neighbour as you probably will never do otherwise. So, there was Pratt, all courtesy and fun, and Harrison, delighted, though hidden secrets of responsibility and anticipation gnawed at him, and Lintott, manliest, wisest of adjutants, and Millward just returning from an 'internal economy' walk round the companies, and myself half lost in the happiness of being thought useful and even then justifying it by plying the handle of the gramophone. 'How's Colonel Allardyce?' 'Well, sir, a five-nine nearly spoiled his bath yesterday — he sends you his regards, he's sorry he blew your front line up the other night, but as you know there is no instance in this Division of a gun firing short. . . .' ' "Crazier Bray" once more! "I'll have the matter attended to, even in the cannon's mouth." ' 'Yes,

54

that's what young James said (he's nineteen), "The trouble with George, sir, is that he suffers from extreme youth". — Augur!' 'Sir!' Enter Augur with his jacket off, grey shirt-sleeves rolled up — pleasant attitude of standing at attention vaguely shadowed. 'Is Mr. Pratt's signaller having his supper?' 'He is sir.' 'Good. Now, Rabbit, recite your favourite poem from Alfred Lester. Or Horace. Or one of your own. He's a shy fellow, this Rabbit.'

If the gramophone handle were abused and ceased to have its natural effect, the interruption in the music did not last long. A good battalion could do anything short of smoking German ration tobacco. Sergeant Seall, though his main concern was with runners and messages, knew all about disobedient gramophones, and soon restored the instrument to begin revolving afresh this overture, that gavotte, that comedian's jest about fire-engines and railway porters. There was no mutability in it; it defied casualty. I shall expect to read one Sunday in the *Observer* a passage like this: 'Amiens. A peculiar ghost-story is reported from Auchonvillers. M. Henri Delabière, clearing some beanhaulm near the old Crucifix, was surprised to hear, as though from a land drain, the strains of a gramophone. Under the impression that a joke was being played on him, he returned to the village; but the next evening passing the same spot, he again heard the mysterious notes. M. Delabière proceeded to Mailly-Maillet and communicated these occurrences to a lady in that town, who took occasion to visit the scene at the same hour, and, having some knowledge of English, was able to pronounce that the principal tune was named "If You Were the Only Girl in the World". Indeed, Mlle. R—— recalled that this very song had been sung to her on more than one occasion in the year 1916, while she was in charge of an estaminet at Doullens, patronized by the British soldiers. Whence, however, the music now heard near Auchonvillers was caused, she could not explain. A full report of the matter is being drawn up by the Phantomological Society of Amiens.'

No; it is all still. The gramophone that went with us from Bethune to the Somme battle and thence to the Convent at Ypres — one of many thousand itinerant musicians of those days — is obsolete. I must discipline myself in this question of winding up clocks and tearing off the sheets of my calendar. There he goes again, 'One Hour of Love with You'; and we are about to return from Mont Noir to the Menin Road in the collapse of 1917, and the floodgates of heaven (is that sour sky heaven?) are open, and the battle is to continue. 'I'd give the sunshine to gaze in your eyes.' Why did they like that amorous ditty at that sunless moment? I found it unsatisfactory, and I still do. I must protect myself. After all, this is not my gramophone, nor, whatever its history prior to 1919, is it our own authentic, distinct, separate, original instrument. On the whole I think that at an auspicious minute I will give the handle one turn too many. Probably G. will not again feel an impulse to repair the relic. I will contrive not to ask him to do so.

(1931)

A BATTALION HISTORY
(with apologies)

THE Southdown Battalions' Association dines annually at the Brighton Aquarium, doubtless startling the regular inhabitants with its boisterous cheerfulness. At the last dinner something occurred which also startled me. It was publicly proposed, and so far as I could observe it was generally demanded, that I should write the history of one at least of these Southdown Battalions. In a spirit of mingled cowardice and devotion to duty I found myself rising to accept this 'onerous honour' (the evening was far advanced); and I now present my old friends with something which nominally tallies with their request. Unfortunately it is shorter than they expected, but the war was also shorter than they expected.

The 11th Royal Sussex Regiment, otherwise the First Southdowns, otherwise Lowther's Lambs (and of course the Iron Regiment), being composed principally of Sussex men, was formed at the outset of the war, but was not sent overseas until March, 1916. On March 5th the battalion landed at Havre. A week later, in the usual fashion of that period, it left billets in Morbecque for trenches at Fleurbaix, in which it received instruction from the Yorks and Lancs. The first casualty (a man killed by a bullet) happened in the communication trench on the way in. Within a year, those who could speak from experience of Fleurbaix, the convent wall, and the suspect farmer ploughing in view of the Germans with white or black horses on different occasions, were rare. The day after the début, possibly because of too conspicuous parades, some company billets in Fleurbaix were suddenly shelled with accuracy and the battalion lost sixteen men killed and wounded.

By March 20th the battalion, its rapid probation over, held a trench subsector by itself; after its four days there it emerged through quiet Estaires to Merville, then undamaged, and spent three weeks under training there. 'Training' made a considerable part of the war's burden. The battalion next marched through the plain southward to Hingette, a hamlet on the canal west of Bethune, well away from the trenches except for some primitive ones that intersected the fields, intended to be ready for some strange upheaval. An eastward move soon followed; billets at Gorre were quitted on April 19th and muddy trenches at Givenchy were taken over. Here the side-effects of the quarrels south of the Canal, in the grim contorted country by Loos, were felt and paid for in some casualties. May-day arrived, and that night the battalion was relieved. Among the willow-shaded lanes of Hinges by the Canal beyond Bethune, it passed several days; much cleaning-up, much *parlez-*

vousing, and on one evening at least, the Band playing. Thence it marched away on May 9th to le Touret, in the rain, and from that straggling hamlet it supplied working-parties until on the 14th it relieved the 13th Royal Sussex in the moonlight along the breastworks of Festubert. A famous name! but May, 1916, was anything but the repetition of that dreadful one of the previous year, which had sown the marshy grounds we dug in with skulls and equipment. In this Festubert locality of snipers and machine-guns we manned our posts and patrolled and wired for almost a fortnight, and when the Hertfordshires had relieved us we returned hopefully to the Hingette cottages and lofts.

But suddenly on May 28th, amid fearsome rumours, the battalion was ordered up to the front line south of the La Bassée Canal, at Cuinchy, which was a 'hot shop'. Here it was that the first Military Cross was awarded to one of us (Lieut. H. S. Lewis), followed by the first Military Medals (to G. Compton and W. Booth); the action concerned had occurred in no-man's-land at Givenchy. The business of the trenches at Cuinchy was strenuous; heavy trench mortars fired often into us, and on June 3rd the Germans sent out a fighting patrol which only succeeded in bombing a few posts. Next night a mine was blown just ahead of our front trench; in spite of the miscalculation, the explosion and the savage shelling that immediately lit up the wet darkness cost us six killed and thirty-seven wounded. The battalion might have suffered

even worse casualties had an unprepared raid on
the fortifications opposite (which was to have been
made by us) been attempted; but it is understood that
Colonel Grisewood, at the price of being removed from
his command, rescued us from this menacing plan.
From the Cuinchy trenches we were withdrawn for the
usual short rest at Annequin, a village of colliers and
pigeons, and we came back early on June 8th in small
parties. This front-line tour produced two more
mines, one German, one (the more imposing) ours;
these did us no harm; some bombing matches took
place where the two trench systems almost joined.
We were now promoted to the dignity of instructing
the 8th Warwicks. During the night of the 11th an
Argyll and Sutherland battalion took our place and
we very wearily returned to Hingette.

North and south of the La Bassée canal were, and
are, when you know them, different countries. We
next went north again into the agricultural country,
lay west of Neuve Chapelle for several days and at
night were busy with picks, shovels and trench
carpentering towards Richebourg l'Avoué. At midnight on June 21st we were relieving the 12th
('Second') Battalion about Ferme du Bois, and in
those breastworks and muddy ditches we remained
until the 28th, when by daylight the Cambridgeshires
came cheerfully in to relieve us and we were scattered
in detachments among the keeps of Richebourg St.
Vaast. Major G. H. Harrison about now succeeded

to Colonel Grisewood, and for a time he had the
continued services of Captain Wallace — a splendid
soldier — as adjutant. Meanwhile, we were informed
of the opening of the Great Offensive of 1916, and of a
local share in it. Down the road, a canvas representa-
tion of a projecting corner of the German parapet,
known as the Boar's Head, was rigged up, and our
storm-troops were practised at it. The Boar's Head was
to be bitten off on June 30th, mainly by the other
battalions of our 116th Brigade; but from our battalion
large parties were detailed for carrying and some
bombing. We knew little of the aims of this attack, and
in our view it appeared a much greater thing than it
in fact was. It seems to have been intended to delay
some German troops and artillery from their march
south to the Sommeschlacht. The attack was advertised by a preliminary bombardment from our
batteries on the afternoon of June 29th. We looked
across at the flying woodwork and earthwork of the
German line. On the next morning, while it was still
dark, both artillery groups let fly (ours had a few
seconds' start), and our infantry went over. The
German machine-guns had no difficulty; the Brigade
and the supporting pioneers and Engineers were
massacred, our own casualties being one hundred and
twenty killed, wounded and missing. Among the
survivors were some, such as G. Compton, who had
gone deep into the German lines almost alone.

Next afternoon, while this kind of thing was being

enacted through miles and miles of Picardy, we were relieved and came to Lacouture, or the orchards that fringed it. We lived partly in light huts and the hours were punctuated by the fire of the heavies. On July 6th at night we were surprised to find ourselves marching south (and incidentally breathing tear-gas). We slept briefly at Beuvry (then a place that pleased us much), but next day advanced through the pale rain, in parties of six, along the stone highway east. The 4th King's Liverpools willingly made room for us in the trenches before Auchy, which were seldom free for an hour from the stinging blasts of all sorts of bombs and shells. Our casualties were all too many. This strain on the nerves lasted a week or so, and we were glad to be sent up to le Touret once more. On July 20th we held the Ferme du Bois line again, and on the 23rd a raiding party was sent across, but its failure cost us seven killed and wounded. Next day we side-stepped into the Festubert breastworks, and held them in high summer weather, when even the War took a siesta, until the 29th. It was daring to try a relief here in broad day but it came off, and we assembled after it at le Touret among the chicken-runs and estaminets. Then, to the general rejoicing, several days of billets in Bethune were given us. The people were kind and the food was cheap. Some may have visited the Red Lamp area, but not so many as would do in many War Books. After this holiday we occupied the trenches at Givenchy again, and made good use of the sunshine and the canal by bathing in the afternoons, about 200 yards from the nearest Germans. Some of these tried to fraternize one morning. Their opening joke was an allusion to bully beef and biscuits; but at that time we were well fed even in the trenches. On August 11th we left Givenchy for what had been long foretold — our part in the Battle of the Somme.

The period thus concluded was quite a distinct one. Throughout the battalion was seldom at any distance from the trenches — but the trenches were in the main 'truly rural'. Horrible and destructive moments occurred, yet there was something of beauty and of health in the general impression. You soon came into the scenes of ordinary life as you left the front line behind. The ruins of Richebourg St. Vaast, of Festubert and even of Cuinchy and Givenchy were substantial, and bits of architecture, gardens and plats attracted us even beyond warning notice-boards about 'daylight movement'. We were now to become acquainted with a mood of War which permitted no half-measures and no estaminets on the communication trench.

Marching well west of the battlefield, we saw unusual sights such as the aerodrome near Auchel, and I think a military mineral-water works before that. We were in high spirits, knowing nothing of the actualities we were making for. On the 13th we reached Monchy Breton, a dank village in the Arras

area, out of which we marched for training on some
breezy downs chequered with thick woods. Here was
ground said to be just like that we were to attack in
reality. Minute instructions were given, and followed
by all ranks. Early on the 24th we were on the road
again, and our march was assisted by a short train
journey; the night we spent at le Souich ('Oh, *swish*'),
and six hours dusty tramp next day brought us to
Warnimont Wood at two in the afternoon. Reconnaissances at a front-line village called Hamel, on the
River Ancre, detached some parties on the 26th and
27th, when all moved to P.18 or Mailly-Maillet
Wood — a dishevelled little scrubbery viewed by
German observation balloons and shelled unpleasantly.
The battalion transport shared the wood and suffered
from the shelling. After making its forward preparations, hindered by much rain, and after two postponements of the attack, the battalion filed into its
assembly trenches on Hamel hillside by midnight of
September 2nd. At 5.10 on the 3rd the attack began.
The gunfire was heavier than we had known. I
believe no one can say what happened to our bombing
parties under young Lieut. French, who was to clear
up the suspected German dugouts in the railway
cutting. Nor is there much detail of our main waves.
Led by Captain Northcote, a number of men went
past the German front trenches, and formed an
isolated post. The majority, under Captain Michell
and 2nd Lieut. James Cassels, dug in nearer the

E

German parapet. .Nothing could be done to relieve the attack, which had collapsed north and south as well. The order to withdraw was sent in the afternoon but Northcote and his valiant companions were not successful in their attempt to recross no-man's-land. The battalion (relieved by the Cheshires) assembled in a trench along Hamel village street and in the setting sun arrived at Englebelmer, three hundred fewer in number than when it passed through that village the evening before. Temporary organization in two companies instead of four was found necessary. The survivors seemed scarcely to realize their survival; it was a dizzy end to an incredible day.

On the 6th we moved, no great distance, to Beaussart, where there were a few civilians whom the men distrusted. Reinforcements from England — four hundred men — were received here. Colonel Harrison rapidly restored the battalion to its normal working. On the morning of the 14th we took over the extensive trenches before Beaumont Hamel and once in appeared unlikely ever to get out. However we were for the present secure from the painful chaos of fighting a few miles south. In these trenches (supported by the decaying positions of Auchonvillers) we worked hard and were shelled and trench-mortared not too violently most days; but the minenwerfers caused casualties. Gas-shelling on September 23rd may be noted; at that date, the only box-respirator in the battalion was at headquarters. To assist the troops in the attacks on Thiepval, southward, we put up rows of dummies in screens of smoke. On October 4th under a burst of shelling we were relieved, but only in order that we might make a circuit through Engle-belmer Wood and Martinsart Wood on our way to the Hamel trenches. A party was sent up during this short interval to reconnoitre the region of Thiepval Wood, which was at that time intensely contested. Hamel was better. Moonlight nights threw a strange illusion over the Ancre valley, and autumn afternoons glowed among the wildflowers along our communication trench, Jacob's Ladder, which began at the poisonous spot Mesnil. The battalion occupied a front usually held by two battalions, and did this safely for ten days. A smoke barrage was produced by us and the trench mortars on October 12th to call off German attention from an attack south of the river. The Royal Naval Division relieved us on the 16th, but we immediately moved into Authuille Wood south of Thiepval and prepared for an attack. When the battalion occupied its assembly positions in the frosty muddy upland, on the 20th, it had been roughly five weeks without rest, and was greatly exhausted; nevertheless, at zero hour (12.7 p.m., October 21st) it advanced over the open with beautiful steadiness to seize Stuff Trench. It did what it was ordered to do, and held the trench until relief at midnight on the 22nd. The cost was two hundred and seventy-nine killed, wounded and missing. Among the killed was an especially cheerful and determined officer named Doogan. The state of the ground traversed by the battalion was extraordinary, and the mud-pools were strewn with corpses.

After the relief, some poor tents south of Aveluy Wood seemed remarkably comfortable; but on the 25th the battalion was holding the line again (Thiepval Wood), and thereabouts it stayed, digging and carrying and being shelled, until the 30th. That morning it worked its way through heavy rain and a slough of despond past Thiepval village to Schwaben Redoubt. Here there was always some shelling, but on the 31st we were systematically bombarded, and when we were relieved (next day) the tour had cost us thirty-two casualties. The relief was expensive mostly to the Cheshires, whom the Germans saw coming in; the business, though simple in itself, took five hours. We rested in the cabin-like dugouts called Authuille Bluffs, on the steep rise from the Ancre inundations, and then did even better by getting back as far as Senlis. Two days, and we were at Thiepval Wood afresh, but quickly returned to Senlis and its barns and estaminets; on November 7th we were working in a winter storm in the Aveluy region, and on the 10th we resumed or were resumed by the Schwaben Redoubt, which was by now a few deep dugouts and a maze of crushed and choked trenches. We attempted a raid the night following, and by good luck caught two German soldiers without losing

anybody. It was beyond the understanding of the
men in the mud that an attack by us was imminent,
but that was the fact, and on November 13th other
units of our Division passed through our positions and
overran, or overwaded, the German forts beyond. Our
task should have been the melancholy one of carrying
and dumping wire for the Division in front of its
extreme advance, but there was such a blaze of shells
bursting in no-man's-land in such a vile November
night that we were let off and had to go no further
with the materials than the old front line. This was the
close of the battalion's Somme battle. One night at
Pioneer road (huts along a sunk track), one at
Warloy-Baillon (unspoiled houses with curtains and
door-knockers), and then on the 15th a march of
fifteen miles ending at Doullens. A train journey
north, on November 17th—18th, removed us from the
Somme area.

There one may define the end of the second part of
this short history. During almost three months the
battalion had been practically always under fire, had
held trenches for scarcely tolerable periods and shared
in three bewildering and devastating attacks. It had
been cut off, with little exception, from common
sights and scenes of life, and had become accustomed
to two views of the universe: the glue-like formless
mortifying wilderness of the crater zone above, and
below, fusty, clay-smeared, candle-lit wooden galleries,
where the dead lay decomposing under knocked-in

entrances. The battalion had vastly changed in its personal composition under these prolonged tribulations; of the four hundred men who joined at Beaussart even, a great number were dead, wounded or otherwise vanished before we left the district.

In piercing cold the battalion occupied M Camp among Belgian farms and the huts of refugees, on the Poperinghe-Watou road, and refitted and drilled there until December 5th. When we left M Camp, it was not to try our fate at Ypres as we might have surmised but to find out still quieter places than Poperinghe. We went by train to St. Omer and by road to Moulle, near which place we built rifle-ranges. On December 15th, however, there was a train journey ending at the ruins of the Asylum, Ypres, and a turn in the trenches north of that city — Canal Bank. This period was one of the most peaceful and harmless that we ever had in the Line. On the 23rd we were sent back to E Camp in Elverdinghe Woods, and a snowy and joyful Christmas followed, in spite of the reconnaissances that day in the trenches of Boesinghe. There we relieved the 10th South Wales Borderers on the 30th, and the year 1916 ended for us in a dull commonplace trench day.

The Belgian Army were on our left flank at Boesinghe, where the front trench was cut in the raised Canal bank. So was the German trench over the frozen shallow Canal. Behind us was shapely clean country, and Elverdinghe Château was intact. We were encamped in its neighbourhood for almost a fortnight before a new and memorable experience — a first night in Ypres, to which we came after dark. Some were in the cellars of the Convent, others in basements near the old Station square. Next night we went through the Menin Gate to relieve trenches at Potijze; fierce cold prevailed and heavy snowfall. After four days 'in', we were relieved by our friends the 14th Hants, and sheltered in the same smoky recesses of Ypres, and went in and out for wiring and other work. Eastward again on the 24th — and we had hardly relieved the Hants and settled down to freeze in peace when a box barrage of minenwerfer shells and whizzbangs cut out our extreme right (a strong bombing post). The Germans had thought out a clever raid; their raiders apparently huddled in a culvert, under the railway by which our post was placed, until the moment of entry. Our men (it was evident later) fought hard, but we lost three missing, five killed, others wounded; three of the raiders were killed. The following evening a false gas alarm called down a bitter bombardment, and the next evening another false alarm produced a similar clash. There was great unrest, and we did our best to scour no-man's-land at night; and it was earnest winter weather. The guns and planes were restless as we. The 14th Hants succeeded us on the 28th, and we clanked down the road into Ypres, for more fatigues in the snow. The Germans raided the Hants next, and though we passed a further spell of Potijze (February 1st—4th) without such shocks, after we had gone out by train from Ypres to Vlamertinghe we still provided supporting companies in Potijze village, and reconnoitred emergency and alternative routes over open land to the front trenches. A German attack was apparently feared.

The Vlamertinghe camp was useful for battalion drill (where a hop garden had been), and vast quantities of fuel were burned there; on February 16th we entrained at the Cheesemarket, Poperinghe, on a little railway which took us to Bollezeele. Great cheerfulness ensued, and the winter relented at last; but such times sped by, and on the 24th we were at Winnipeg Camp, Ouderdom, on our way into the Salient again. Next day we moved to Ypres and Zillebeke Lake, a reservoir in the Bund of which were dozens of flimsy dugouts. Headquarters was a tall drab house at Kruisstraat, memorable to us as the last headquarters of Colonel Harrison while he was with us. Here he received an order to proceed to a Staff school in England. Almost at once the battalion suffered more troubles. The adjutant, Captain Lintott — brilliant in the Somme battle — was compelled by illness to leave us. Then when the battalion, after a terrific struggle through the dark and storm, occupied trenches on Observatory Ridge, it was bombarded and raided, and lost sixteen killed and wounded. Among the casualties was the regimental sergeant major, Daniels; a shell burst in headquarters at Valley Cottages during the relief, and he died a few days later at Vlamertinghe. A great man.

Leaving Observatory Ridge, its bony stumps of trees and naked tracks, on March 3rd, the battalion was some days in Winnipeg Camp, and reconnoitred a reserve system at Dickebusch. It returned to Ypres by train but on nearing the town waited for a furious bombardment to slacken; once again it took over the Observatory Ridge trenches from the 14th Hants, amid bursts of rain and gunnery. Four days on the grill here, then four with night work at Kruisstraat, then Winnipeg Camp again, then the short train ride and the halt while Ypres was being further pulverized, and Observatory Ridge once more. This time the four days ended with the headquarters being driven out of Valley Cottages (a most dangerous solitary set of ruins) by the German gunners, and trying to find some better hole in the scarcely preferable raggedness of Zillebeke. This search the 14th Hants continued, during the night of March 31st; the battalion retreated into Zillebeke Bund. The snow reappeared, and betrayed the secret entrances to the dugouts of Observatory Ridge, where the battalion again took charge for four days. Emerging on April 7th, we found an alluring 'revue' being played by the 49th Divisional Follies in a vast hut at Brandhock, but as we drifted forth from it into the crystal light of evening we saw and heard a display of artillery in the St. Eloi direction which 'beat all'. Trouble was anticipated for us, and indeed for everyone in the region; but the German attack was limited and local. There were days in the Infantry Barracks at Ypres (stiff with big guns now); at Brandhoek again, among the farmers; and then in the wet the battalion manned trenches about Hill Top Farm north of Ypres. From these it moved back to the Canal Bank, then a sort of Garden City of pretty dugouts and many of them. The end of April approached, and another Allied Offensive was also thought to be approaching. We entrained at Ypres, passed through our old M Camp, entrained again on May-day and formed up outside St. Omer's distinguished-looking station. Marching on (with one night at Hallines), we found very humble billets in a cow-scented village named Zudausques, and were kept miserably and ironically busy with training in a new method of attack. In this manner May, 1917, went by; but halfway through we were transferred to Wormhoudt, where there is a hotel; but we saw little of it. Inspected and trained to a degree, we next moved by road to D camp in the woods of Elverdinghe.

The Salient was becoming uglier all round. The battalion was helping to build railways for a few days, then held trenches — June 1st–6th — at Hill Top. At all hours spiteful bombardments were put down, and the first day brought fourteen casualties. There was gas on all sides, too, when the battalion came back to the Canal Bank; it was no sort of rest, and the next

trench tour in a heat-wave had countless grim
moments. No place was safe. Those trenches were
not made for this power of artillery. On June 16th
there was a midnight move to Elverdinghe, and on the
21st we went by train from Poperinghe station
(listening to the explosions of shells in the station
yard) to Watten and on foot from that dreamy village
to even dreamier Houlle. This move was one of the
wetter ones. At Houlle we were happy, beating down
much promising corn with our practice offensive,
swimming in the big ballast-holes, and approving the
inexhaustible beer of the place. And this lasted three
weeks and more before the offensive in question
dragged us eastward. We arrived then by train at
Poperinghe (passing new sidings, and hospitals!) and
marched to C Camp, Elverdinghe. It was changed.
Camps shelled, air duels, dumps exploding, new roads,
tracks, light lines — these were the disorder of the
day.

On July 22nd a patrol sent by us to Hill Top under
an inexperienced officer disappeared, complete with
maps and papers relating to the attack. Other patrols
were sent up on later nights. The Canal Bank was
full of gas. There were reports of a German withdrawal, but it was found not to be quite an innocent
one. By night on July 28th the battalion marched into
its assembly area — trenches old and new at Hill Top.
Dreary continuous gunning accompanied us. On
July 30th, waiting and preparing, at least seven of us

were killed and six wounded. The skies had plenty of rain in them, despite liberal disbursements. On July 31st, at 3.50 a.m., as dark as could be, we attacked the demolished High Command Redoubt. The British barrage was such as numbed our powers of realization; the reply to it was instant, but diffused. The battalion took its objectives, and got busy with a line of shell-holes, shaping out some kind of posts; but the rain set in, and what the careful fire of the German heavies did not do the rain did. It rained all night, and through August 1st; and the German gunners, from their reserve positions, fired on with accurate diligence. By 3 a.m. on August 2nd the battalion had gone forward to relieve the 14th Hants in the Black Line, along the Steenbeek; a formidable day followed. Counter-attacks threatened, and were broken up. The German gunners did their utmost for their infantry, and all our headquarters were destroyed by direct hits. From this bad eternity we were relieved at night by the 17th K.R.R., and found our way to the far side of Canal Bank, a hot meal, and what sleep could be got. The blaze of dumps just behind was hardly noticed next day, and nobody was pleased with the prospect of further trouble in the front line; but we escaped that, and by train and road were sent to School Camp, St. Jans ter Biezen, beyond Poperinghe. An estimate of our total casualties in the action was two hundred and seventy-five.

The sun came out, and life improved; moreover,

when the battalion decamped, it was to a fresh area, that of Meteren, the pretty spire of which looked along the highway to the Moorish steeple of Bailleul. Here a sort of divisional reunion happened, and the bands of several battalions played in the crowded streets; it was as though the spirit of the preceding year were challenging that of 1917. A move to Dickebusch on August 12th, and reconnaissances, preceded the return to the 1917 spirit of Spoil Bank (Hollebeke). Midnight at once produced shelling and gas, which affected everybody. On the 17th the battalion went forward into the shell-holes, not knowing where the Germans were (and the Germans were as well informed about it). Four days of that, and two at Spoil Bank again where the instantaneous fuse caused some losses; thence to Ridge Wood Camp, shells and showers. On the 27th the battalion relieved the Black Watch at Hollebeke (the operation took over seven hours); the dugouts surprised even us by their stench. A wind arose and dried the shell-holes, which was much appreciated. After this term of four days, relief only meant the homeless wreck of old trenches near Spoil Bank, but that was followed by some better days at Ridge Wood Camp.

In mid-September the battalion held the line at Mount Sorrel, and carried in materials for an attack; was in Divisional Reserve at Voormezeele; did four days' slogging in Larch Wood Tunnels. In that hideous neighbourhood, while some of the headquarters were waiting the word to proceed away from the line, a shell fell in their midst, killing seven of our best men. The names of the next camps which the battalion endured sound odd — Ascot Camp, and Beggars' Rest. From these withered, draggled places we moved into the true gehenna on the 23rd, and the next evening occupied the front line (no line!) south of the Menin Road. This quarter was called Tower Hamlets. The daytime was burning hot, the night subtly cold, and frantic shelling from 'the Tenbrielen Group' continued. On the night of the 24th a German attack drove in the battalion on our left, but Captain P. L. Clark saved our situation (a habit of his). On the 25th this position fighting continued, and on the 26th our brigade attacked and cleared some ruins of Gheluvelt outskirts. There had never been, in all our experience, such shelling; and the SOS signal went up north and south most monotonously. On the 27th at last one of the shells that hit the headquarters pillbox went through and killed six. How the Rifle Brigade relieved us in daylight, we scarcely knew. We halted a few hundred yards back in Bodmin Copse, and the copse was treated to measured and exact shelling from heavy howitzers. Gas shells came later, but we got away, and that night were carried on lorries from Bus House, St. Eloi, to Berthen, hilly and windy country. The casualties of this Menin Road tour were estimated at 200.

Now the usual restlessness of 'rest' ensued, parades,

cleanings, baths, exercises, and lastly reconnaissances.
Mt. Kokereele was left behind reluctantly on October
15th, and on the way up to the battlefield a shell
dropped among headquarters staff with deadly effect.
In that district there was hardly time, or condition,
for noticing who was dead. Round some deep water-
logged tunnels called Hedge Street and Canada Street
this was particularly the case. The battalion spent
two nights in the Tunnels, then three in the front line,
where once a stream called the Bassevillebeek had
flowed. It now lurked in a yellow swamp. The front
line was calmer than could have been dreamed, and
the tour was lucky. The guns were fighting the guns
rather than us. The German artillery ignored an
SOS call from their infantry who took our being
relieved to be an assembly for attack. We withdrew to
Bois Camp, near Dickebusch Brasserie — a set of
melancholy bivouacs; but we got a little warmer on
October 21st (the anniversary of our Stuff Trench
success) by marching to baths at Kemmel Château.
It is not everyone who has a Château to bathe in.
Two days after that distinction we were transferred to
some old horse-lines near Reninghelst, which
amounted to an involuntary cold bath; the wind
howled and the rain flashed white. Odd jobs followed,
and at least we were promoted to the decencies of
Chippewa Camp on the 29th. From that place we
went forward about October 31st to carry the customary 'materials' and dig a trench beyond Hill 60 — an

operation well conducted (Col. Millward's head-quarters were in Larch Wood Tunnels, one of the finest works of the kind). There was a lavishing of gas shells and general 'ironware' on our tracks; but on the morning of November 1st we were met by lorries in St. Eloi and so 'home'.

The name 'Tower Hamlets' had a pernicious sound for us, but to that point of the firing line the battalion was sent next (Nov. 3rd). Its chief performance was to throw smoke bombs, assisting operations at Polder-hoek Chateau just north and Passchendaele farther off. A harmless relief followed, but when the battalion had gone as far back as Bodmin Copse a single shell killed three officers and N.C.O.s (I make no attempt to register all casualties; this is by way of example). On November 7th the battalion moved farther back to Godezonne, *vulgo* God's Own Farm, Vierstraat; and in the succeeding days it went, *via* Chippewa Camp and plenty of rain to Bedford House, a mud-spot near Ypres. For the rest of the year 1917 the 11th Royal Sussex were mainly employed as workmen, under the direction of the Royal Engineers or our own Pioneers. A few days — November 25th to 29th — were granted at Winnizeele, almost civilization; on the 29th the battalion took a train at Godewaerswelde to Ypres. The train made good time, leaving at 8.55 a.m. and covering the dozen or more kilometres by 10 a.m. Encamped on the Potijze Road, the battalion built lengths of railway and causeway; all might have been friendly but for air raids. At 5.30 on the evening of December 6th, one bomb killed eight and wounded eight. These men thus missed the agreeable return from St. Jean station (a scarcely believable sign of the British advance) to Winnizeele and thence to the barns of Seninghem. There in spite of the eternal training programme and rifle-range, Christmas was, as they say, celebrated; on Boxing Day there were snowball fights.

The year 1917 ended with the battalion in Siege Camp, by Ypres. Siege Camp was left for Morocco Camp, another bleak place with a view of Passchendaele, of no touristic value. In rain and snow, from January 16th at dawn to dark on the 18th, the battalion held a few advanced mudholes at Westroosebeke. Trench feet (a crime) became a serious concern. For about a week the battalion remained in Hill Top Farm, among its memories of old trench tours and the initial Passchendaele attack, and in School Camp. A big move was in preparation, and, having entrained at Proven on January 26th, 1918, the battalion arrived after twelve hours at Mericourt, in the south of the British line.

Thus ended the battalion's principal connection with poor Ypres and her sad Salient. It had been a lengthy connection, and one which we should have wished to end sooner. It is true that through 1917, when we were not in the line, we were sent often enough to a considerable distance from it, and passed

F

weeks in sleepy villages and safety. Moreover, philanthropy from above frequently caused one or other of us to be dispatched to one of the courses of instruction, far from enemies, that multiplied through this year. But the dreary dreadfulness of front line experiences now, the sense of a curse over and round Ypres, the 'looped and ragged nakedness' of forward camps, the air war on them, the apparent futility of the British effort, and the shattering of all unity by casualties beyond our counting, made that year at Ypres a bad business.

Invigorated by the prospect of a new front that, whatever it would be, was not Ypres, we moved forward past Peronne. By light railway, in a fantastic scene of trees bearded with hoar frost, and a ghostly silence, we came to the Cambrai battlefield and the ruins of Gouzeaucourt on a hill. We worked this sub-sector, between Revelon Farm as close support and the firing-line with its useful deep dugouts and keeps, until March 12th — about thirty-six days; and a great deal of digging, wiring and carrying was done besides the actual maintenance and defence of the positions. Originally calm, the place became noisy and deadly — there were tragedies on the duckboard tracks. On March 9th, crossing the wide no-man's-land, D Company entered the German trenches and found nobody. At last the battalion was taken out, and was busy for a few days finding its way about G.H.Q. Line, in Gurlu Wood and Hem; it was at Hem on March 21st. *Dies*

Irae. Then came the Germans. The story hereabouts feels the strain. On the 21st–22nd the battalion was fighting and withdrawing at Villers Faucon, on the 22nd–23rd on a ridge near Bussu, then along the Somme Valley and across the river at Buscourt, and at Hem on the 24th. Reorganization at Chuignolles (March 25th), a withdrawal near Harbonnières (26th), through Harbonnières (28th), a Divisional concentration at Cayeux (noon of the 28th) — these are the dry bones of this episode. Then on March 29th the battalion faced the Germans at Wiencourt, withdrew to Ignaucourt, to a sunk road north of Aubercourt, to another south of Courcelles; on the 30th, it was driven back in the early morning and gradually retreated to the Villers-Bretonneux—Aubercourt Road. A fine position was taken up before the Bois de Hangard and improved at once; then on the last of March the 18th Division relieved. To collect what remained of the battalion was the next task, at Cléry and Amatre. The action had cost 20 officers, 300 other ranks killed, wounded and missing. On April 7th the unit marched twenty-five kilometres to Embleville and on the 9th entrained for Arques near St. Omer.

But rest was not yet. Ypres even was not done with. A day or two at Tatinghem, and there was a railway journey to Vlamertinghe. Toronto Camp, Otago Camp, and another march to Voormezeele, with its ugly associations. Here the battalion began a new trench system and had soon the chance to test it, the

Germans (after several days of cannonading) attacking it early on April 25th. The shelling of Elzenwalle Château ruins was tremendous, and it was there that headquarters had placed themselves. On the 26th the battalion re-took from the Germans its old friend Dickebusch Brasserie. There were new alarms, assaults and barrages next day, but the King's Liverpools relieved that night, and the 11th went into support near Dickebusch Camp. The noise of battle, and more than noise, involved it even there, but it had a night or two at Devonshire Camp. On May-day, the battalion relieved in the front line. This tour ended on the night of May 3rd, and so far as I know that was the last time on which the 11th Royal Sussex as such had any concern with trench tours. By way of St. Jans ter Biezen and M Camp, well known resting-places, it was withdrawn to Nielles-les-Ardres, near Audruicq, which again is quite near Calais.

There the battalion was split up. Part of it was given the honour of instructing American infantry, and afterwards served in the mysterious campaign in North Russia. Arctic kit was finally handed in, and the whole history ended. Ended? Not while the Southdown battalions meet, as annually they do, to preserve their co-relationships. In sketching the movements of the 11th Royal Sussex overseas, I have hardly referred to the personalities who most of all would be mentioned among us when we gather now. I hardly know how to do it, without doing injustice to many others on whom,

consciously or unconsciously, we relied. Let me remember Lieut. Swain, our unbeatable quartermaster,
and one who was ever with us though not of us, our
Brigade Commander, General Hornby. In my rapid
chronicle there is nothing about the life and labours
of our Transport, who never once let us down (we ate
our iron rations at Stuff Trench, but there was some
misunderstanding). Of the impressions we had, of
every place and time we knew, I could not unprompted
give a fair general account now; some we have merci-
fully forgotten in the main, others we have a trick of
remembering. It is all so long ago now; and yet when
I think of the 11th Royal Sussex on a winter evening,
under all its ordeals or in any of its recreations,

Bare winter suddenly is changed to spring.

(1933)

PART TWO

JAPAN

JAPANESE MOMENTS

AMONG the privileges of one who for a few years 'occupied the Chair of Lafcadio Hearn' at Tokyo, that of being invited to expound things Japanese for those who are in prospect of teaching appointments in Japan is agreeable but perplexing. Apart from the problems involved for the individual in transferring himself from one end of this overcrowded world of work to the other, his chances of returning to any appointment in this country, and so on, and whether he thinks of remaining in the East for many years, there are general aspects which arise, and veil themselves in moving shadows. Perhaps they reveal themselves in the best seasons. Does Japan disappoint the stranger? What is the young generation like? What will be expected of me, and what shall I take with me?

Japan does not disappoint the stranger; she corrects his fancies, perhaps a little grimly, and then begins to enrich him with her truths. The Japan of the towns is not a promising spirit at first view:

> She is no phantom of delight
> When first she glooms upon our sight.

The galvanized-iron age invades that land of niceties. The concrete store and the fishmonger in a kind of hen-house next to that vast importation do not equal even our shopping streets for comprehensive charm. The little temple is so dingy that one longs for the familiar dinginess of the Unitarian chapel. The canal looks very like that gruesome one outside Ypres in the decomposing summer of 1917. The trams, if moving, bump and crash past, with half a dozen labourers hanging on to the brass rail at each door; but stoppages are frequent. There is a firework display in the evening, and glorious it should be; but ten thousand pairs of slouching clogs fill the area with dust, and you barely survive. You have seen Japanese conjurers daintily performing; but, on joining the thrusting circle in the park corner, you find an outlandish man swallowing and regurgitating with dreadful strain a large brass ball. I mention a few details at random out of the many in which a Japanese city makes itself felt. The worst side is perhaps the meeting with dogs and cats evilly diseased and apathetically driven on to their release. Bewick's *Waiting for Death* is nothing to it.

But for all that, one can praise one's life in a Japanese town. There is a lessening of the tyrannies of the West. Things you *must* do — exhibitions you must see, museums you should know, athletic events you should attend, historic places you should visit, new literary masterpieces you should discuss — are not so numerous as to cease to be valuable. You can manage them, and are attracted by them when they have their day as you wish you had been by others elsewhere. A few dozen scraps from the studios of French artists arrive and are on view; your students see to it that you go with them, and you walk slowly in your socks round the simple rooms, aware that you are making the best of your luck. Presently the Japanese exhibitions come on. How perfect in their way the old school are, with their sepia and their pastel effects! One understands better now how mother-of-pearl is made by a still older artist. The new painters, with their endeavours to outmonster the monstrosities of uninspired futurists, are of course . . . But you have looked at their pictures. Your students listened to your comments, which indeed were rather frequent. You have spent a happy afternoon, within its limits. Nor will these rhomboids and tomato sauce give you bad dreams. You go to the museum. You have seen the sumptuous collections of Japanese arts and crafts at home; and here there is a comparative dearth. But you look longer. You are in Japan, and taking root. That autumn moon, that mountain, that hermit are addressing some sense in you that has been obscured. It is the sense of contentment, verging on the mystical.

When you go out into the country, the mystical hint is not strong at first. Perhaps you are kindly desired to make one of a party of students and professors. The train pulls up at a long platform with a wooden hut or two; you pass out, leave the little alehouses and biscuit-counters behind, and tramp along the road between the ricefields, and up the hillsides. The talk is pro-

bably about the drama (*mem.* to read *The Apple Cart*).
At length the desired 'famous scenery' is reached;
there are benches outside a tea-house, the dried fish
and fried eels are produced, a little lager is procured,
not much is said, cameras are out, Professor Z is induced to put on a false nose and moustache and his
photograph is taken. A storm rolls mightily over the
immense green and voiceless plain below. The forests
pass the word. The waterfall, too, is saying something
where its still shape whitens the rock. You are not in
a book, but you are under a spell.

The young Englishman, employed in a Japanese
centre of education, may find himself out in the
country, where even the din of a Japanese department-
store would be welcome. I remember one such, who
was indeed without much assistance. Few moderniza-
tions were in view. There were only one or two
Western persons for miles, and not many of the Japanese there could converse in English. He compared the
three years ahead of him to a tunnel, too long to show
a glimmer at the other end. The question even of obtaining suitable food was difficult. He triumphed. It
was an adventure, and, as a Japanese gentleman said
to me when I complained of these changes from the
rich life of an English University to the isolation of a
country village far beyond Yokohama, the English are
said to be adventurous. Now, looking back, my
friend's district was rather like Flanders — tags of
hamlets, flat, parcelled close-worked lands, no flowers

to speak of, nowhere to go. His cottage, a peasant's, was like a billet in the Béthune marshes.

But there was a naturalness as worth discovering as that of Flanders, and a loyalty and zeal not unfit to be compared with those of our former 'active service'. The loyalty of a Japanese is no news. It is only from those who are offended with Japanese pride that the notion of untrustworthy Nippon is circulated. These people are not the 'good servants' that may be found among the Orientals. The Japanese are not Orientals. They are as distinct from the Asiatics, if I may be bold in a generalization, as Saxons from Portuguese. But, to resume the track, young Japan is capable of an intense and aspiring regard for a mind genuinely labouring to be of assistance. Scrutiny on that subject is serious. Those quiet eyes and polite bows do not mean that judgment is wanting. It will be favourable, in a way that hardly exists in England, if patience and endeavour are seen. That drowsy, heavy youth who comes up at the end of the morning with some query (precisely what, it is hard to hear) on the biography of Mr. Galsworthy, or the length of a Yule-log, will be grateful for a careful answer, which he goes off meditating. In a year he will be a cheerful, not unconversational visitor, unwrapping from his silk handkerchief — by that time his teacher has begun to use one instead of a portfolio — a copy of some newly acquired book, or a Japanese clay figure for the *sensei's* table.

And there is an accumulated force and movement

in this approach of young Japan. There are cross-currents, it is true, of a jealous nationalism, and a kind of lethargy sometimes creeps in, necessitated, it may be, by the great burden of education forced on boys who must acquaint themselves first with Chinese characters and presently with our widely variegated language and one or two of the others. But the air of that country, traditionally kind to mental and spiritual careers, is still cultural. Conscious that there are worlds to conquer, the Japanese student sets about the campaign with a seriousness that sometimes hardens into mechanical dryness, but usually is like a blossoming. His interests not being over many, he wishes to think. He certainly does not take enough recreation, but baseball is played more and more, and one is not anxious to see the balance swing too far in the direction of 'half-time scores'. He suddenly identifies himself with a great author as far as he can. Poetry is no idle fantasy to him, although Japan has never had poets of the type that transform life. He hails those who have done so elsewhere. He sits in the café (which someone has assured him is perfectly Parisian) and converses with a kindred soul (in kindred Harold-Lloyd spectacles) on the true meaning of Browning's *Sordello*. The passion for our literature, interpreted with the knowledge of a fellow-countryman, resembles our own passion for Greek and Roman glories. England has become a new Athens to many Japanese. Our foreign policy may be counted a nuisance; our efforts in war, in science, in commerce may be thought inferior; but, in a serenity apart, our imaginative inheritance is honoured, and its radiance gives light and energy.

Mr. Laurence Binyon will have done much by his expedition to reveal our own paintings to the Japanese, whose habit of mind it is to credit to each nation a monopoly of one form of achievement. Our art has seldom been able to peep round the corner of Italy and France. It has been partly our own fault. We do not commonly think how stern a fact ten thousand miles are, and, if we cross them, we are in want of much that was left behind. It is not necessary to be systematic to a degree. A recent candidate for the Japanese adventure came to me with most beautiful lists of equipment. Was Badminton played? Croquet? Lacrosse? At this I thought of a story which one better versed in Japanese life than I am loves to repeat. He was visited at the end of the holidays by a very healthy and well-built young man, one of his class, and he asked him what he had been doing with his holidays. 'I was playing,' replied the innocent student, 'with my little sister.' The best thing that a man could take to Japan would be a dozen cases of ordinary English possessions and another dozen of books, prints, music, and whatever reveals or is taken to reveal the intellectual genius of our race. Then everyone would be satisfied, the exile would not feel the length of his tunnel so oppressively, the inquiring mind seeking the correct number of nails in a horseshoe or the history of

the Oxford Movement would depart in bliss. Here, a
simple story may speak clearest. 'What is this, *sensei*?'
'That's a shoe-horn — a little ancient.' 'Is this the
ordinary English shoe-horn?' 'It is . . . Would you
like it?' Smiles, and 'We don't see these in Japan . . .
I am very much obliged to you for your kindness.'

(1930)

A TOKYO SECRET

THE old man sitting at his low table within the entrance of the shrine of the Seventh Tokugawa, where the clamour of Tokyo streets dares not yet enter, pensively received our admission tickets, and welcomed a little conversation. November airs were taking short cuts through the building, and he admitted that it was a cold though an honourable post, from eight in the morning until four in the evening; shortly he would be allowed a *hibachi*. It was the want of incident, however, which (one gathered) emphasized that naturally pensive expression; 'Nobody comes, some days, and I have to sit here alone'. Of the few who did visit the place, scarcely any, he said, were foreigners.

There are so few beautiful and sequestered loitering-places in modern Tokyo that the apparent neglect of the Mausoleums at Shiba by the foreign population is a little puzzling. Perhaps we all overlook what is close at hand, in our faith in things at a distance. Whatever the explanation of the old doorkeeper's loneliness is, there is good reason for reforming the case, for, once within the boundary walls of the Mausoleums, one breathes an air of tranquillity and solitude. There is space as well as silence, and great trees overshadow

G

noble old buildings. The birds know the ancient security of the scene, and their careless conversation is heard above, thin, confused, but well pleasing. In harmony with that, the decoration of the walls and doors is rich in wood-carvings of birds, enough to test the efficiency of the young Japanese ornithologists, while the carvers' equal profusion of branch, flower, leaf and thorn must delight anyone who knows his botanists. The dust of the highway and the touch of time have dilapidated some of the exterior craftsmanship, and the colours, the crimsons and the emeralds and sea-blues, have sunk into partial oblivion. But (with the exception of a few unlucky birds' heads and wings) the design remains in all its engaging multiplicity. There is something of the fairy tale in all this ingenious and mysterious ornament. Perhaps none of the birds, the animals and monsters would be here if they had not a symbolic duty to do, to speak to the initiated of abstract joys and virtues and aspirations. But, even without reading any such secrets, one is allured by the fantastic forms of that world of wood and paint.

There the unicorns gallop and frisk with a mood between pleasure and anger. A unicorn's moods are bound to be somehow unique. Long reptilian dragons, rather like lobsters from another universe, swing their enormous heads backwards, as cats run races with their tails. Lions which no one could pass off as thoroughbreds, blue, green and clay-coloured lions, display their frequent coils of muscle, bite the ground, claw the air, or stare with twisted necks into the sky. Their eyes are indeed expressive eyes, but we shall never know what it is they want to express. Innumerable warty heads thrust themselves out of the shrine's inner walls, and we compliment ourselves on recognizing them as elephants, with gilded tusks and most inconvenient trunks. Below, vividly tinted even in the dim religious light of the shrine, a series of birds amid flowers is said to hint to us what Paradise is. The dove and his mate seem to possess those blossoming plum-trees, those deep red peonies by grace of the Tokugawas whose three-leaved crest reappears at every turn. Dove-like, above the porch, or on the ceiling, angels float through time. One sounds her flute, another her guitar, a third her drum, and all are singularly like those celestial musicians seen in the seventeenth-century work of English churches.

The birds are mostly not so supernatural; indeed, many of them are admirably portrayed from the life. One cannot swear to that in the instance of the phoenix, whose golden vanity struts on a number of the lacquered panels, but the artist has not forgotten to put a sparrow with his cock and hen; to leave his yelping eagle in royal solitude; to perch his small parrots in affectionate nestling nearness on the bough. Small and great, his birds form a charming variety, nor are the canopies of leaves and flowers, the stones and streams where they are placed less various. Lotus and iris, plum and peach, pine and azalea at once catch the eye, but other graceful blossoms and stems are there in the ancient labyrinth of design. So giftedly simple is the carving that even with the flowers in the outdoor pieces one does not lament too strenuously the decay of 'the colours fresh, originally bright'. Behind the folds of one of the doors, two particularly fine examples of the artist's choice of essentials may be found, the subject being a waterfall with its crags and its bamboo and maple; and though wood scarcely seems the material in which the water-fall's intense action should be expressed, yet here one marks the broad unbroken torrent pouring down the cliff and with a little aid of the fancy one hears the roar of many waters.

But these are the details of the place, attractive perhaps only to the few; without taking a close view of such incidentals, a saunterer in the courtyards and corridors here should yet feel all the better for the interlude.

'How reverend is the face of these tall shrines!'

Around them, like a guard of honour, long columns of bronze and stone lanterns stand marshalled, and by their multitude alone command a sense of eternity, or at any rate a philosophic remission of the noisy problems of to-day. Nature herself has a retreat here; the plantain and the thistle have their corners, the climbing bine may bring to perfection her little gourds like pendants of coral. It is a refreshing thing to find a place, in this packed and envious capital, where common weeds and shrubs may encamp unmolested. Even out of the walls, some green shoots hopefully emerge. They have evidently the leave of the door-keeper. The Mausoleums themselves, in their dark lacquer patterned with dusky gold, rise solemnly yet not at all dismally above their peaceful precincts. Perspectives of vermilion and golden arches unite doorway with doorway, and richness appears in the intricate concatenations of ornament on every pillar, ceiling and gable. The Tokugawa crest in its circle is nowhere omitted, and yet it does not advertise itself. By strong flights of stone stairs, one mounts to a coign of vantage, undisturbed save by an occasional old woman passing to sweep, and thence the view of the greenish fluted roofs, the well-massed memorial build-ings, the wide and unfrequented approaches, with leafy lights and shadows stirring round about, is serene and ample. The busy crowd over at Zojoji are clattering in the grey dust to and fro; the lorries and cars go bumping along past the outside gates; but here one is willingly under a mild enchantment of quietness.

(1926)

WINTER COMES TO TOKYO

THE vine climbing over the bamboo fence and the little tree I called a laurel had withered, but the three quince-shaped, quince-coloured gourds which she had so gallantly given to a wasteful world continued to cling there with mysterious constancy. A fascination stole over me, as I looked on these golden fruits so curiously suspended. Day succeeded day, dropping at length precipitously into darkness, and as each said farewell, with brief crystalline eastward glance, I said farewell to the lingering simple trilogy in the garden, and slid my shutters with the inevitable difficulty and din of that duty. In the morning, there were the dauntless shrivelled vine and her fruits again; and at last I began to think the calm perpetual, and that I had found the world's best climate.

When at last the fruits had shrunk and rotted, and with sudden venom winter came in at the many chinks in a Japanese house, I was shaken out of my trance. A horrible oil stove and a beautiful brazier were brought in, and it soon appeared that appearances deceive, for the oil stove communicated genuine warmth, the brazier a faint though fuming degelidification. The wind blew sharper, and in my dreams I was frequently reporting for duty among wild shapes of war in snow-strewn morasses. And now I found myself on the horns of a dilemma -- no new thing, but none the better for that. As thus: I had written to my old friends of my Japanese house, and they had returned answer to me, imagining most industriously my comings out and goings in: was it fair to have given them all that trouble, and then to leave the house because of an inconvenience or two in temperature and air-passage? Meanwhile, the north wind reached my heart, and I went off to an hotel. Snow, thaw, frost immediately followed, disproving the statement of several old Suffolk friends (instinctive experts on meteorology) that the climate of Japan would suit me marvellously.

Do I seem to be complaining? No doubt; but I am not the only one in this 'vast municipal jungle' who dislikes the climate, and who talks about it, or even who does something about it. The street scenes, which ordinarily have their curiosities, are now wintry enough. The solemn and long-unshaven citizen lifts his feet and their wooden platforms along through the slush with a difference. He wears around his neck a little fur tippet — often what looks like a complete rodent; and his ears are concealed in natty little tufts of fur. There is something in the design which sends my thoughts away to *Buffon's Natural History*, with plates. Our Yedo worthy also has a liking for a muff, uniform with the ear-tufts; and he repels the insidious germ with a little black gas-mask neatly fastened to the face.

Meanwhile the season of fires is at its height. The ferocious siren of the engines is the *nocturne* to which one is obliged to listen again and again, and, as this howling message multiplies through the livid air, the watchmen come under the windows with their rhythmic simple music, the clinking sound of their staves beaten together, and add in bleak accents the whereabouts of the fire. Tokyo is in the main a wooden city. One tries to be sure of the name of the street which the watchman is crying out, and one's geography is not allowed to grow rusty.

Life in a small Tokyo hotel is not so strange as it might seem, nor so romantic as Lafcadio Hearn would even now paint it. Man gets to work in the morning, and returns at evening; woman works most of the time. A Japanese novelist lives a floor above, and I, a rustic scribbler, here; we are unacquainted; the psychologist who said 'professional jealousy' was quite astray. Time slides away so quietly, so Japonically, that one's best intentions are symbolical, not actual. Of eight aspects of Buddha, one is easy enough. I sit in the calm of ages, while the windows (glass windows) rattle in as glacial a breeze as curls now round the gateway of Gray's Inn: unless, perhaps, some of my neighbours set about their evening *samisen* practice. There is a remarkable book about Japanese instruments of music; I have been cooling an intention to read it for months past; but, judging by the circuitous noises which I have heard lately, I cannot be

sure that the *samisen* is entitled to a place in that en-
cyclopaedia. Really I must look it up. And I am not
sure whether I ought not to begin thinking about
mosquito nets; the winter will no doubt melt away,
and the vines run up the fences and swell their golden
gourds, while the thinking is still simmering gently by
the horrible but accustomed oil-stove.

(1925)

ON SOME HUMOROUS PRINTS
BY HIROSHIGE

WHEN we speak of Hiroshige, we naturally think of the artist who with bold simplification and endless design expresses the characteristic scenery of Japan; the mind is occupied with such triumphs as the great eagle hovering above the icy river, the yellow moon stealthily appearing at the end of the gorge, the white rain hissing down on the desolate river and solitary boatman. There is the artist who speaks, without need of a translator, to any quiet mind in any country of the world. But there is another side of Hiroshige, unimportant but not unworthy of attention; the lighter side of caricature and caprice. Since such a useful historian of Japanese prints as E. F. Strange of the South Kensington Museum only makes the briefest allusion to Hiroshige's humorous productions, it may be no work of supererogation to describe a few of them which are not often met with. There is nothing astonishing in their quality, nor do they suggest that Hiroshige if rightly understood might be ranked with Phil May as a comic artist; but they have their individuality.

Dilemmas, practical jokes, witchcraft and hauntings — these are the subjects in general. The first picture to my hand is gruesome enough. Three women are shown at their toilet, one using a powder-puff, one combing her hair, and one blackening her teeth; but instead of faces we see that these women have vegetables — one a monstrous melon, another a head of maize, and the third an egg-plant. This metamorphosis has come apparently without warning. Below the picture (there are two on a sheet) is a more flippant drawing. A boy and a girl, their mouths gaping with grinning expectancy, are lurking behind a water-butt. The boy has put out a purse on the end of a string. A passer-by, peering through spectacles, is stooping to pick it up. On the water-butt may be read *Yoku-shin-cho*, 'Quite a New Way'—some local allusion. The mischief of children provides the subject for the next two pictures, in one of which a clerk is seen dozing over his ledger and his order-box. Behind him is a punning inscription, meaning, 'This is the letter-rack' and also 'Look at this wreck'. The clerk's dream is drawn floating above him — a large dinner. He smiles in his dream. Meanwhile a boy has opened his ink-box and taken out the brush, with which he paints extra 'eyebrows' on the sleeper's face. The companion-piece depicts a writing-school. The master's room is seen through a door. In the absence of the master, two boys have piled up the old-fashioned desks, and one of them has climbed to the top, mantled in a large copy-book, the folds of which stretch out like a dragon. As the master enters, he holds out his tongue and raises his eyebrows in such a grimace that the old man falls to the floor with hands raised in bewilderment. To heighten the effect, the boys have daubed a grotesque, staring face on the writing-book which hangs on the wall.

Momotaro, among other famous beings, finds a place in this gallery. He stands behind the counter of a street stall, selling *kimidango* — advertised as 'the finest in Japan'. The pheasant comes to buy, dressed as a woman, and is shown receiving a double share; but there is trouble close by where the dog, firmly grasping his portion of the food, is being assailed 'with yell and blow' by the monkey, who means business, and reaches out a robber's hand. From this we turn to a piece of jovial irreverence; the Thunder God has fallen to the ground outside a shop with the sign 'Repairs for Ribs of Umbrellas'. The merchant, wielding a sort of trowel, is apparently asking the capsized deity if he can do anything for him. The rain drives down, and the thunderer's drumsticks lie in the mud.

Some of these prints are meant to suggest that the way of the transgressor is hard. In one, a couple of ruffians are drawn peering through the lattices of a bath-house, and so absorbed that they do not notice the *saké* running from the overturned jar which one of them was taking home, nor the dog making off with the cutlet of devil-fish which was to have gone so well with the liquor. Another situation of the sort is noticed where two apprentices, one a fishmonger's boy, the other from a fried-*tofu* shop, are going for each other tooth and nail in the street. One boy brings his left to bear on the other's nose; his opponent is pulling a handful of his hair out; but whichever wins, both have lost, for a dog is slinking away with the fishmonger's *bonito*, and two hawks have raided the *tofu*.

But why should the errand-boy in another picture come to grief as he does? He has been sent for *saké*, and on his return with three jars and a keg has been stopped by an ourang-outang and a tortoise (creatures fabled to be addicted to drink). The ourang-outang, a strange fiery-haired half-human, has his foot on the sprawling, bellowing apprentice, holding him down while he drains his second jar (the third grasped in the other hand waits for treatment). The tortoise is look-ing after the keg, and as it is held almost upside down he can probably manage it all himself. Such a fancy needs no moral. The fabulist nevertheless dominates some of these drawings introducing animals. Human fashion and pride are probably smiled at in the draw-ing of three cats in the blue and green costume of the *nō*-dance. Two have fans inscribed 'Pussy Crosses the Bridge', and these assist to hold up on end three lengths of dried *bonito*, which Japanese cats delight in. The third cat, wearing high *geta*, carrying not only a fan but an umbrella also, steps neatly from point to point of the awkward bridge. 'The biter bit' is illus-trated in the following simple way: a fox hides behind a rice-stack with a line in his paws, ready to pull tight a noose in the middle of a trap. The trap is baited with a purse. A hunter, his mouth open wide in anticipation, is about to reach his hand to the purse.

Such are these humorous sheets by Hiroshige. Sometimes his broadness degenerates, and one is forced to hurry past a picture — there is one, for instance, making a savage joke of a couple of blind men. As for the technique of these pieces, there is no need to say much; most of them are casually drawn and coloured, with a chosen ugliness of feature and limb, too extreme to be enjoyed. The animals are, like so many in oriental pictures, marvellously unlike any animals in nature; a 'cat' with a stroke of the brush becomes a 'dog', a 'dog' coloured brown is a 'fox'. How Hiroshige should be content with this ambiguous nonsense, it is hard to see; but one finds some very odd beasts in European natural history books as late as two hundred years ago, and until general feeling towards animals becomes affectionate and liberal, old conventional ways of drawing them pass as good enough for the occasion. The heart controls the eye, and without that light all is out of drawing.

(1926)

'LINE UPON LINE'

THE magical minuteness of Bewick, recording on a few square inches a tragedy or comedy of country life with detail upon detail to enforce the sense of truth, giving us in a few tiny yet fearless strokes the foliage of a particular tree, the age of a stag, the temper of a dog, the very hiss of the slashing blizzard and the enormous guffaw of a blacksmith enjoying a cruel joke, is ancient history with many of us. The difficulty of amassing the 'facts' and conjuring up at the same time the *genius loci*, which has latterly driven poets in the several arts into strange postures of perplexity, pessimism and 'revolution', never occurred to him, and never occurs to us his much obliged servants. It is unlikely, too, that Cruikshank often found himself afraid of the problem; we can therefore respond to the unmistakable commands of his engravings when in the emotional mood, or we can at our leisure explore their nooks and corners for the pleasures of old customs and bygone circumstances, and be richly rewarded. We know where we are, and we see the incidental curiosities as well. In the excellence of this subsidiary truthtelling, the names of Bewick and Cruikshank are perennially partners with that of mighty Hogarth, whose infallible eye for the life itself must have been as

sharp as Lamb's — and that was understood to be
almost able to pick up pins and needles. 'Hogarth's
graphic representations,' wrote the essayist, 'are indeed
books; they have the teeming, fruitful, suggestive
meaning of *words*. Other pictures we look at — his
prints we read.'

Lamb read, besides his Hogarth, the fairy tales of
old China with such delighted perception and sweet-
sounding chronicle that one laments the dispensation
by which no example of the Japanese colour-print ever
arrived in England in his day. For surely he would
have found in this art also 'a flowery tale' with countless points of varied life, designs of intellectual fantasy
affording many a vista and exquisitely lighted glimpse
of men, women and manners. The artists of ancient
Yedo also had the secret of drawing their subtle dream
of form as well as the tangible, diurnal equipage of
their mortal span. The 'floating world', which gave
their artistic tradition its name, was a clear and gentle
stream of bright reflections, infinite variations of
necessity and habit. They are wonderful chronologers,
costumiers, furnishers, coiffeurs, what you will, and
congenial with the British masters of variety in unity
('how all's to one thing wrought!') who shared their
actual period. It is true that their idea of the particular
is hardly so intensely fine as that of Bewick; there is a
generalization about it, with all its accuracy, understandable by a brief consideration of Japan even now,
where the beautiful and dexterous and delicate detail

of existence is as a whole iterated with a certain monotony. But in their degree (and it is not easy to exhaust their fertile field of attentive intimacy), the Japanese print-masters are a library of historical truths almost as much as a pageant of daring or aerial shape and jewelled colouring.

It is simple as it is heart-easing to test the resources of observation which enrich, without overwhelming, the Japanese print. I take up the latest of my small assemblage, bought hurriedly in an east wind and harsh flaring light from a street dealer — a 'pavement artist' in his special way — and I find it apt. It is a print in three panels, a pattern in jet black, light brown, and grey-green. The immediate effect of its chequering masses of blackness, its slender curves of figure and robe, is the pleasant one of life without hurry, enthusiasm without noise, peace without monotony. These ladies are indeed graces, this house a haunt of peace, and one almost inevitably speaks in a gentler tone in presence of the mirrored past. The painter is Toyohiro (1773-1828), and his honoured name loses nothing by its appearance on this achievement. But for the moment my mind runs upon the extraordinary mosaic of pretty truthfulness, the number of tunes which ring in the ear of fancy, throughout the three plates.

This seems to be the daughter of the house who is sitting, 'for ever young', on her cushion in a corner of the balconied room. Her hair, arranged in a tall, ballooned, anointed superstructure, with comb of tortoiseshell before, and coral ornament behind, announces her distinction and pride of place. Her gown is hung with large tassels, and diversified with ivy and other leaves. On her right is set the brazier, its two pokers fixed close and perpendicular as they should be in the sand round the charcoal — the brazier-box is lacquered and inlaid, and two other lacquered boxes with a pattern of tendrils creeping in gold over their sides stand by it. One is her 'escritoire'; the other is at the moment crowned with an incense-bowl. On the lady's left, a little maid-servant in plain dress with the wide open sleeves proper to childhood, and the formal high *obi* or girdle, sits demure and patient; and by her again sits a waiting-woman, with the same steeply piled, glazed hair — no, not exactly; her hair is brought to a kind of summit, and she has no comb nor ornament, other than four undecorated projecting hair-pins. A box of folded fans, with their paper clasps still round them (for they are new), lies open before her, and she has taken one up, and is slipping the clasp from it.

Behind these figures, an angled screen occupies the visible height of the room. Hereon we see a hilly place, on which a stormy and fantastic peacock, spreading his ample tail, eyes a humbler peahen; pillowy conventional clouds hang about them, shrub-grown rocks and the heavy buds and blossoms of the peony complete the setting. The lady sits, one dimension nearer

life than that picture in a picture, and with one hand
poising her patrician chin seems lost in admiration of
an open fan which she holds; upon it is a design of a
chubby girl, who is more than she appears to the un-
initiated — she is the Girl of Good Luck. The fans in
this part of the picture are of more than customary
significance, and we proceed in Japanese style, from
right to left, in order to work out the simple riddle.

The centre of the room presents the dominant factor
in the balanced play of black masses through the print,
and at the same time the chief actor in the scene. The
full black coat of the seated gentleman there at once
attracts our notice. We cannot be sure, to judge by
physiognomy, whether he is a gentleman — no reflection is here made upon his nature or behaviour, but
he answers to Elia's description: 'I love the men with
women's faces'. His family crest, a leaf of the maiden-
hair tree, spreads its little white fan on his sable sleeve.
Leaning forward, he applies a large brush to a large
white fan. His lacquered paint-box, in four tiers,
stands near; miniature bowls, evidently for pigments,
are ready for use in the top tray, but three are not in
their recesses — we catch sight of those, on the floor.
Three saucers are next to them; for he is using three
colours, his deep black, his grey-green, and light brown.
Small brushes and other things await their turn on a
black square tray; a round black tray holds his two
bowls of water.

Three fans spread somewhat carelessly on the floor

just out of his way testify to this young man's charming technique. He is a second Toyohiro. One of the sketches reveals a man with a bald head resting on a sack, filled out with what we may guess to be rice. This he has probably earned, instead of money, by means of the monkey, dressed up in jacket and hat, which he keeps at the end of a cord. One would like him better if he did not carry a goad in his right hand. The next fan is grotesquely limned with a large shell-fish and draggled seaweed. On the third is a flattish flower-pot with a dwarf tree in flower. A fourth fan is in the fingers of a waiting-woman; it shows us the spiky, crooked branch of the plum-tree. This lady's black dress is sprinkled with a pattern of laurel leaves; a companion's is adorned with those of the maple; and another, standing over them, has chosen cherry-petals floating in rippled water as her flowing kimono's glorification. She is unrolling a drawing of an excessively hairy, pig-nosed, gaping monster, who brandishes a sort of switch used in Buddhist worship — from what legend has he escaped? One fears lest another like him should find his way to the blank roll of paper placed at the convenience of the artist.

Beyond the balcony swirls a shallow stream, such as we mostly see in Japan, and the ubiquitous pine-groves plume the little hills on the farther side. The water flows with our inquiring spirits into the third part of the picture. Here, another waiting-woman is sitting, in attitude to receive from one standing a lacquered tray (of the tendril-decoration observed elsewhere), with sheets of blank paper intended for future fans. Yet another maid stands by, holding two larger rolls of paper such as will one day be 'hanging pictures'. The dresses continue to be beautiful. We see here an *obi* with the symbolical design for waves, and the curious traditional ducks upon them; there a coat of the prevailing black filigreed with pine sprays and streaked with the strange finger-shaped mists of conventional landscape art. The dignity of the house is once more hinted, as it was in the screen at the far end of the room, in the heavy tassels which hang from the sun-blinds rolled up above the balcony and the daylight.

(1926)

BUDDHIST PAINTINGS

THERE is an undeniable fascination in the rooms of the Imperial Museum at Ueno where a number of ancient and acclaimed Buddhist paintings are on occasion assembled. One need not be a profound inquirer into Oriental art in order to feel the atmosphere of these solemn presentations of belief and piety, or hierophant and deity; only one must master and for the time being expel from the mind one's definitions of art and existence. The plain fact is that a Western mind cannot grow enthusiastic over this strange, unimpassioned and inconsequential kind of painting on a sudden; it obviously counts as 'an acquired taste'; and there is no hope of the ordinary spectator's recording his impressions of it in that spiritual treasure-house where the visions of Rembrandt, Goya, even Ruysdael gleam and give comfort and revival. But his ultimate return from these Buddhist masterpieces to a world of art in which he flies from blossomed bough to fleecy star with the wings of fancy and grace and reality does not obliterate the fascination which they have had for his dreaming mood.

It was the touch of hallucination, the drifting light vapour of dream and unsubstantial distance, which distinguished for me a group of these paintings at Ueno from the others. On entering the exhibition, I found before me some portraits, dated between the tenth century and the fourteenth; these did not communicate to me any subtle ecstasy or unusual significance.

The picture of Jion Daishi (from Nara) showed a man with a jowl somewhat Napoleonic, an eye with some of that meaning associated with Cardinal Wolsey; the red mantle expressed this strong personality in the manner of its drawing; but altogether I felt no gift in the artist, that 'I should wish to see more of him'.

Or again, there was the likeness of the youthful Prince praying for the recovery of his father; admirable here was the poise and patience of the suppliant, finely serious the mantle's green (as of deep lakes) which threw into prominence the ornate and sparkling censer in his extended hand. Yet there was no echoing voices 'of old, unhappy, far-off things' for me in this decoration.

The crude liveliness of another adjacent picture, showing a Chinese priest, with long finger-nails preceding the famous set of Ah Sin, with darting eye and punchy lips, merely impressed by its fresh appearance. In the background of the painting, idealized flowers floated sweetly, signifying that angels were hovering near in delight over the priest's homily; but from those sharp features one found it difficult to imagine a sermon 'which drew an angel down'.

But, proceeding in ordinary course through the rooms, I soon found that infusion of a daydream which I take to be of finer worth than the bold daubings just spoken of. The Kyoto triptych of 'Kwannon, Monkeys and Crane' has no horrid, deliberate, waxwork accuracy; immediately on seeing it, one knows that the artist was a considerable mystic. His name was Mokke — 'a Zen monk who thoroughly understood nature'; it is said that he was a prophet without honour in his own country, China, but vastly appreciated in Japan. And well he might be appreciated. Here, in this triptych's central panel, below a willow, in a mountain solitude, mild Kwannon sits with folded arms and slightly inclined shoulders. She recalls the 'pensive Nun' of John Milton's poem.

> There held in holy passion still
> Forget thyself to marble.

Beneath her hermitage, a river wells and widens, emerging from a romantic chasm. This is a remarkable expression of musing and divine haunting; nor is it unworthily companioned by the side-panels of the triptych.

On one of these a crane is crying beside a dim mere, its water almost indistinguishable from gathering mist. This crane is certainly 'done to the life', and (in the ordinary phrase of appreciation) we can hear the wild cry; but what the artist has succeeded in painting is that occult motive or desire which separates birds from

human beings. His crane is crying about something—
but we are excluded from that secret. It is noted in
this drawing. On the other side, the long-handed
monkey on a bough is also to be suspected of some
meditations special to himself.

Such an intimation of secrecy — one might almost
say second sight — seemed to me to be the principal
virtue of two landscapes perhaps seven hundred years
old, and attributed to the Chinese Emperor Kiso.
The spectator as he comes to these pieces is, I think,
immediately filled with the effect of immense height;
to that notion is quickly added a spirit of reverie.

One of these drawings (black and white) images an
autumn scene; a recluse is sitting on the bank of a
mountain path, looking steadfastly at distant clouds;
and the impression is that he sees and hears some
mystic envoy. This rapt figure is a kind of comment
on Coleridge's magical poem 'Kubla Khan', and helps
us to see how

> Five miles meandering with a mazy motion
> Through wood and dale the sacred river ran,
> Then reached the caverns measureless to man,
> And sunk in tumult to a lifeless ocean:
> And mid this tumult Kubla heard from far
> Ancestral voices prophesying war.

The companion picture is a winter-piece, in which
the hermit turns in his travel along the snowy mountain path, below a crag where the willow strains in the

wind, and a chilly torrent, struck by the sound of a monkey's cry. That cry is famed as one of the invariable sources of deep melancholy among the Oriental poets.

Two other exhibits which have this same hint of timelessness and aerial pageant are the property of the Imperial Museum. The official 'Handbook of the Old Shrines' has lighted on some most mysterious language in which to promulgate their genius; 'the composition as a companion Kakemono is well designed, and the gradations in shading are varied enough to lead the spectators on to the feeling pervading the whole canvas. The forcefulness of the strokes characterizes the whole picture'. Perhaps it does, but there is more than technique on view here. There is a pervading spirit of solitary musing, which deepens until one starts in amazement to find that a branch is tangible and solid: the mountains and waterfalls here are on the borderlands of what old English romance called Faerie, and the voice of the streams hushes into an undersong of pure content.

It is in these fine, reserved, yet rich works that such an exhibition makes its most genuine appeal to one accustomed to the myriad evocations and hints of western art. The rest is not silence, it is true, but what is it beyond quaintness, peculiarity and mere antiquity? (I must not omit that tireless dexterity which has made such accurate facsimiles on screens, of peonies and such flowers; but where do we rate Fantin-Latour, or 'Bird's-Nest' Hunt?)

One may spend agreeable moments before the rest of the pictures, and be exercised with the activity of Homo Sapiens, if that is still his correct designation, and his willing faith. I can certainly recommend these extraordinary elephants, lions, tigers, which not even Lord John Sanger ever caged, to those who do not know them; and it is a pastime to identify the mammals, reptiles and so on, in a charming act of worship to risen Buddha. The immeasurable groan of the bear can hardly escape notice. Some of the scrolls unrolled in the cases below are fantastic, such as that which relates adventures of two priests in search of certain sacred writings — they plunge below the sea, where preternatural swordfish prance in excitement, and arrive at a submarine palace guarded by a porter with a coiled serpent as turban, for a king with a medium-sized dragon as his crown.

(1926)

ATAMI OF THE PAST

THE day had been one of those which pass much too quickly, and even as they delight us have a hint of a mocking smile. 'Hark, again that dreary chime!' Not that one actually hears the chimes at Atami, which does not westernize at top speed. We heard the racket of the printing-machines of the local newspaper, of course; we were bumped along in the motor-bus; and the brutal clamour of motor-cycles drove us into the drains of the narrow shopping-streets. But to an alien sense, the principal characteristic at Atami was the innumerable exhibition of cuttle-fish hung out like linen on lines to dry before every cottage — an odd sight, and (to be frank) an odd smell.

We took due notice as we went out of the village to the cliffs, whence the sea was seen to hoard opalescent lustres and glitterings, to flaunt violet and forget-me-not wave-blossom, and hawthorn foam-flowers, to covet the green darkness of midsummer woods. There, the pine trees stubbornly look over their watery estates, or crawl drowsily down the rock like giant lizards.

This scenery enjoyed, and wondered at, we returned to do justice to the fame of Atami's hot springs by personal experiment—to wit, bathing in them; and though swimming in hot water is a trifle tedious, justice was done. The loitering sea below the balcony of the Japanese villa turned to mother-of-pearl, the volcano's twinkling smoke over shadowy Oshima came and went; then greyness chilled the air and dulled the harbour, and we found all too quickly that we should have to hurry for our train.

In the train N., who is an ingenious explorer of the book-stalls between Kanda and Waseda, attempted to beguile us of our regret at the close of a peaceful interlude by translating from an ancient pamphlet an account of Atami a hundred years ago. In 1830, to be precise, his author had written his description; and feeling that Atami in the past would be a picturesque place, and hoping that ancient metaphors would worthily express our modern response to its serenity, I ventured to take notes from the interpretation.

The traveller, whose pen-name was Kyosanjin, appears to have suffered from pains in the back, and in search of relief he left Nihonbashi for Atami in July. Part of the way he walked, and part he rode in a chair. He arrived, and noted that before Atami the sea spreads like a fan, and behind it the mountains rise like a screen. He put up at an inn, and gives a list of twenty-one inns in the town; he informs the public that rooms may be rented at any time, and cooks may be engaged locally. His advice is that although it may sound extravagant to go to Atami, the truth is quite otherwise, the inhabitants being of simple character, and the waters beneficial. The ailments for which he recommends the springs are such as withered hands and feet, the palsy, eye diseases (seven days will get rid of them!), cramp, beriberi, contusions, piles, sterility, toothache, bad circulation, abscesses, asthma — one imagines that he will catalogue all the troubles of the flesh, when he breaks off to say that persons with leprosy and dropsy are strictly forbidden to enter the baths.

His sole anecdote of the efficacy of the waters is on the authority of his landlord. A woman had had no sleep for the trying period of six years. Ten days after her coming to the Atami baths, as she was at break-fast, after three mouthfuls she let her chop-sticks fall, and sank down in a deep sleep, which lasted (as well it might) for three days and nights.

In case his readers were not allured sufficiently even by that story, or perhaps had not even the tooth-ache, Kyosanjin was careful to draw attention to the various recreations of the town. The cinema, baseball, billiards, as yet were not; but he was not at a loss on that account, making up the following graceful if rather dreamy sports programme — Japanese chess, Tea ceremony, Lending library, Archery, Shell-hunting, Firefly-hunting, Trout-fishing, Listening to the cry of the deer, Listening to the singing of insects, Mushroom-gathering, Pheasant-shooting, Snowy weather. To that we may add Massage and Medita-tion.

The pleasures of landscape and the southern sea, as a whole, scarcely struck this author. He mentions Hatsushima, but only to fancy it as a whale floating on the waves. Oshima, which he compares with Asama-yama, interested him principally as the island of strange women, who, as the villagers of Atami affirmed, neither blackened their teeth, nor shaved their eyebrows, nor put up their long hair. They wore a kind of chaplet of silk or cotton, which showed to what class they belonged. Kyosanjin enumerates the mountains, rocks and wells around Atami, but without comment, except when he describes the powers of a certain 'Parrot-Stone', five miles up in the hills — it answered perfectly the songs and chatter of jovial persons happening to camp close by.

The trade of souvenirs must be one of the oldest in the world. In 1830 the visitor to Atami was cajoled into buying articles of camphor-wood, tobacco-boxes, trays, cups, incense-holders, soup-bowls, saké-bowls, special strong paper, hot water bottles, and of course views of the place, which may have been no more representative than a familiar gaudy example by Toyokuni, with the sails of ships beyond Oshima rivalling that island in height, and the indigo bay improved almost into an inland sea. The largest kind of souvenir was perhaps a barrel of spring-water, which the tourist might have forwarded for him by sea to Yedo.

The guide-book, like most of its race, would impress

127

some antiquarian theories upon us, and explains the origin of Atami's springs at some length. In the reign of the Emperor Jinken the sea at this point began to produce boiling water. Shoals of fish were unfortunately cooked in their native element, and presently the corpses began to smell so strong that people refrained from coming to Atami any more. However, when the Emperor Tenchi reigned, a priest from Hakone went that way, noticed and regretted the fate of the fish in the boiling waves, and offered prayers on the subject. A venerable old man appeared, who told him that the hot spring which killed fish would cure men of disease, and that it might with advantage be transferred into the mountain. The priest set about this task with resolution, and after three days of prayer and fasting, in the night he heard a noise like thunder among the hills, and saw the sea running high. Coming from his cave on the shore, he found that a vapour like a white cloud was rising from the hillside into heaven. This vapour still rises, not so dramatically but to the admiration of all comers, from the spring called O-yu.

(1926)

GHOSTS AND GROTESQUES

THE colour-prints of Kuniyoshi, though generally allowed to entitle him to an honourable position among Japanese artists of the popular school, do not often meet with hearty admiration; nor is there room for serious complaint about this. Kuniyoshi had a most imperfect sense of the unity and harmony of a great work, and his own pieces are usually good in parts but altogether confused and effectless. To this heavy disadvantage of incoherence, of a junk-shop style mainly unpleasing, nature added a second defect in his composition, his obsession with ugly forms and features. Grace and sweetness, the lyrical charm, the light of happiness enticing all the scene to smile, will rarely be found in Kuniyoshi. His clumsy faces, his rigid trees, his putty mountains and waves too frequently betoken the want of that spontaneous pleasure which gives life to handiwork.

These adverse considerations notwithstanding, there is a quality in Kuniyoshi to be reckoned with. It is his fertility in fancies of the grim or grotesque, not very subtle ones perhaps, but odd enough to attract attention and to keep it. The innate tendency to express ugliness, which has been mentioned, may have been the source of his ingenuity in ghosts, goblins and bad

dreams. The case is not unusual; an artist's strength is
often his weakness. Nobody would accuse Kuniyoshi,
in his series of prints caricaturing the 'Chushingura
Bewitched', of having produced pretty pictures, but
nobody could deny him the success of his busy talent
for the monstrous. In the course of half a dozen
scrawled and daubed pages, he confronts us with a
profusion of diabolic wit. We see respectable citizens
sprouting hen's feet instead of hands, with faces
turned into the heads of catfish, or huge caterpillars,
or herons, or shellfish. Human countenances are thrust
out by tubular necks coiled round tree-trunks. Pine-
trees develop men's faces, startling the samurai
servant so that his eyes swell enormously, his forehead
bulges. A vine bears not gourds but leering heads.
A samurai with eyes like squids receives the obeisance
of a beaked and feathered retainer, while in the picture
on the wall the rocks of Ise are turned into giant frogs,
and from the dusk outside a tremendous, vicious demon
threatens. Even the smaller objects of common life
share in this bedevilling. The ceremonial tray assumes
legs, and walks; the dropped umbrella becomes a
salamander, and the straw hat a clam; the straw-
stack observes these things, being itself transformed
into a hedgehog.

In a set of prints called 'Scenes from the Life of
Nichiren', Kuniyoshi attempts the realization of the
supernatural in its nobler aspect, but it is not his
particular province. One picture shows Nichiren

praying, and his enemies closing in upon him; their ugly work is however frustrated by the moon, which sends down portentous blood-red rays. These rays are not (in the print) as awe-inspiring as they should be. They look like painted sticks. Another moonlight scene is lit up with the apparition of Buddha in a plum-tree, shedding a yellow light, which should be a glory, over Nichiren. For a third miraculous piece, the artist borrows the Great Wave of Hokusai (but he adds his own cold stormy sky beyond it), and below the foaming crest he shows Nichiren and his disciples in a boat, while in black ink the inscription appears in the angry water, 'Glorious is our faith'. And another print illustrates the saint, in the course of a sermon, being menaced by a dragon (till that moment, a woman); it is a springy, lengthy, and distinctly hostile dragon, but too conventional to imply unholy terror.

The series of 'Sixty-Nine Views of the Kisokaido' displays Kuniyoshi's taste and thoughtfulness in finer degree. Here, his plan is to illustrate on the same sheet a chosen place, and an historical or legendary episode associated with it; he gives the landscape in a little vignette or inset at the top left-hand corner, the description opposite it, and below the page is filled with his heroes and his ruffians. I do not think that the heroes and ruffians are worth their place, and the gaudy elaborateness of their part of the picture generally ruins the picture as a whole. But those miniature landscapes above, in their varied framework, are often excellent, their smallness justifying their bright and gem-like colours; and the panels describing each print are enjoyable also, for the artist has given them many shapes and many bordering designs.

Of the vignettes the finest is a waterfall picture, enclosed within a diamond, and simply composed; a sky of fading violet, a green upland with one small house among the trees, cryptomerias standing above the blue and white cascade. In the rich tranquillity here suggested, in the perfection of the mosaic, one sees a grace to which Kuniyoshi seldom had an open mind. The ornaments of his titles too, though they help to overload his page, are greatly to his credit, for they are inspired by genuine feeling, and there seems no end to his store of them. With a Japanese farmer's coat, straw sandals and implements, with a fisherman's net and 'eel-killer', with swords, armour and flags, with fans and candlesticks, with pigeons, with puppies, in short with whatever suits his picture, he interweaves a charming border for his brightly tinted inscription. Accordingly the 'Kisokaido' series of Kuniyoshi, while it may not challenge the dignity and clarity of Hiroshige, has a value and pleasure of its own.

One of the 'Kisokaido' pieces expresses strongly the fantastic interest of the artist. A sleeping samurai awakes to find a lean blue hand, on a long writhing arm, touching his cheek; at his side squats a phantom enemy; and behind — with greater art — the cold midnight mountains assume uncertain likeness of skulls and ghosts. In such work Kuniyoshi is powerful and independent. Other examples of the same eccentric skill are a silhouette piece of foxes, which 'come like shadows, so depart', hovering about with a hint of some malevolent dance; a dancing piece, in which indeed an old man inspired with wine is bounding and capering, while round him a ring of mist-like skeletons share the performance, some playing the samisen and the rest dancing furiously; these, and a less obvious work in the set of 'Products of the Provinces', showing an evening scene, turbulent and bleak, and fowlers netting wild geese. The wild geese in their panic are made to be subtly akin to the dark streaming clouds above, which scud along like the frightened birds, with the shape of huge outstretched necks and straining bodies. And doubtless there are other such works, for the brush of Kuniyoshi is too prolific to be completely known by an ordinary inquirer.

(1926)

THE BEAUTY OF VAGUENESS

WE were standing before a small landscape picture, delicately drawn and tinted, of which the effect was dream-like (so far as it went), a region where things passed like glistening shadows, and the distance hovered uncertain as a morning mist. K., a student who has been long endeavouring to take me seriously, but without perfect success, cast a desultory glance on the piece; turned aside, and after a moment said with a sigh, 'Sir, I do not think you can comprehend the excellence of such a Japanese picture'. I had been fancying that the essence of it was akin to Corot's 'silver-grey dream of Central France', whether it included some oriental religious reference or not; but K.'s verdict on my hopes caused me to look again without such a comparison. My renewed view was as before; the appeal of the tender mistiness, the dim radiances, the lonely hill track and the old peasant with his horse was the appeal of 'Do I wake or sleep?' But I replied to K. in simpler terms: 'You, as an Oriental, think you understand all Western art and literature; surely then the West may perceive what is valuable in your art and literature'. This answer was followed by the cheerful assent of N. and the other students present, and when I had given my notions on the picture, I added the reminder that Western eyes had long feasted on Oriental art, and that many great collections from India, China and Japan would testify to the liberal taste of our travellers. N. very happily observed that between art and art there is no difference, and K., grinning, relinquished the matter. No doubt some hidden associations in the picture above us had urged him to speak; but the manner of his speaking was significant.

For, if I read aright, there is firmly rooted in the Japanese character a belief in the beauty of vagueness, and, arising out of that, a cherished formula that Japan has a spiritual secret so fine and rare as to be quite incommunicable to people of any other blood. Or it may be a still more primitive proposition than that; namely, that Japan must seem to be hiding something from the world. To be understood — to be degraded! The 'wropt in mystery' strain becomes a little monotonous at times.

In public life, the convention of mysteries and secrets appears to be extraordinarily popular. The Government, the police, the army and navy all give it frequent exercise. Newspaper paragraphs elaborately proclaim that foreigners were suspected of photographing secret areas, that the police examined this or that person and are keeping the results of their investigations secret, that the forthcoming poison-gas experiments or manœuvres are the subject of extraordinary precautions against espionage. Even at the

Imperial University one is aware of this doleful esotericism in small matters such as the division of duties, or selection of books for a reference shelf, or a colleague's intentions for next year's course. Indeed in education vagueness goes so far that many students, encouraged by tradition, lodge themselves behind some dark term like 'aesthetics' or 'psychology' and live there illustriously but ignorantly ever after.

In art, it is undeniable that the landscapes done in black and white after the Chinese manner sometimes achieve a far deeper happiness of spirit, a far greater solemnity and majesty than even the best paintings of the popular school, familiar to the world in the colour prints of many masters. There is indeed a sense of mystery in those long hanging-pictures or screens, which are properly appreciated through hours of contemplation, bringing to them a complementary solitariness in which the voice of the waterfalls begins to murmur and rustle from the canvas, and the laugh of the monkey of the mountains, the crow of the pheasant sound aerial and supernatural. Small wonder, then, that these works are esteemed in Japan as of a higher order than the colour-print, which originally was kept in a box, and was not contemplated but glanced at much as one glances at a magazine. But no matter how ill-drawn and spiritless a hanging picture may be, the Japanese still retain some faith in its having a 'mystery,' while usually they ignore the bright curious secrets of style and pattern, even of interpretation of nature, found in hundreds of colour-prints. And when (as is very commonly seen) a room is decorated with a celebrated autograph instead of a painting, it is often, apparently, the illegibility and crabbedness of the writing which the guest hails, with intaken breath, as a triumph of art.

I often wonder whether the strong retention of the Chinese-Japanese writing characters, of which nobody seems able to give the number of thousands, is not due finally to the same creed of the superiority of the incomprehensible. There is no mistaking the gleam of pride with which a traditional Japanese refers in the company of a foreigner to these complicated marks, or the irony with which he stoops to mention the passable ability of some laborious foreigner to write and read them. Taboo operates here. Nippon once more closes her gates.

(1926)

'NOT ONLY BEAUTIFULL'

DIVERGING from the true art and mystery of colour-prints, I shall here pay my tribute to an unconsciously entertaining writer on the subject, sometime employed by a Tokyo firm of publishers to supply the English explanations accompanying their very charming reproductions. These are already exceedingly good value for the modest price asked, but the additions of the interpreter almost persuade me to offer the firm a trifle of conscience-money. At all events so individual a writer deserves a wider audience than the limited number of print-collectors, and he shall have it. He is what he says a certain picture is, 'not only beautifull but also washable'. Witness the following examples:

A Man of high character in his hermitage. By Ba-en.

> Ba-en was one of the prominent artists in the age of Soh, and signed himself Kinzan. He was contemporaneous with Ryokai whose name is too well-known to need nat conventional introduction regrettable to say, Ba-en's biography is unknown.

138

Parrots. By Jakuchu Ito.

[The print shows only one, and that a peculiar 'parrot'.]

Being one of the eminent artists, Jakuchu Ito cut a conspiceous figure in bepaint the hen. In order to paint the domestic fowls to the life he is said to have spared no pains in watching and observing the fowls he reared, therefore his skill in painting them is wonderfully admirable. The artist signed himself commonly Tobei-an, as he used to ask persons one To of rice a coppy of picture as payment.

Joyful Spring. By Iwasa Matabei.

Iwasa Matadei, who is father of Ukiyoe School, was worked in Kanei period. In that time the scholers of Kano and Tosa, proud their style and look down upon the Ukyoe, but they painted without sighn. It is cold that painted by Matabei. His real works show tendency of lantern jawed. The Picture of this volume is said that painted by Iwas Matbei, at all the style, there is little doubt that it was by the blush of some celebrated painter. . . .

Iris Laevigatd. By Suzuki Harunobu.

Harunobu, who is originatler of Nishikie, painted skilfully picture as well as wooden painting differing from other many Ukiyoe scholars who are master in either of them. This picture is reproduced from his original autgraph, so we find round face without grief and fine, deep coloring. He a pupil of Nishimura Shigenaga, was good at painting beautifull woman. He did not paint the picture of actors despising it. He diet at his foerty-sixth age, 1770.

A hair dresser. By Baiyuken Katsunobu.

Katsunobu belongs to a scholar of Kaigetsudo, but his career is perfectly unknown in these days, and it is strange that the picture of this volume didn't take off the manner of Kaigetsudo. This picture is a reference material for us.

Our art critic endeavours to give us 'a reference material' for the various signatures of Hokusai, but is not very lucid, as might be expected.

Our famous Katushika Hokusai had Plenty Popular names and this sign of Tameichi also one of him. demake deep study his art as a puple of Shunsho, in those days he signed Katsukawa Shunro. If we eunmerate his popular name he balls as sollows. Tnnmei 1. jewaaai. . . . This picture is master-piece of Fuji views to be written by him wither Bun sei 12 to tenpo 5.

The great Utamaro also inspires the commentator to freedom of speech and information:

> There is no objection how Utamaro had excellent arton drawing beauty, sure he is a wanderfull artist for East. The old memoir 'Ukiyoe Ruiko' says Utamaro have not ever drow the actor's like-ness but on his yong years he had drew some likeness too and all of them signed 'Hoshō'. This gorgeous picture of slim body beauty is so-called full display of utamaro style it is a wark of his declining years and this one is exposed the room of 'Hinatsuru' Oirān at Chojiya Yoshiwara, beauty dressjhowing the nice Tamagawa Rever at Musashi.

One more, adumbratory of a very fluent, gay and simple pattern called 'Fete Day Dance by Hanabusa Iicho'.

> Hanabusa Iicho was born at Osaka 1652. He gone up to Edo 1666 and then he study as a puils of famouse Kano Yasu nobu, afterwards perfectoey settled down his art for imitate or compromise the art of drawing Tosa school and style of Moronobu's. This painting is one of his most favourite ufiyoe how every bodny dansing with joyfull, one of leading singer covering his face by round-fan and load his nice voice and one is prlaying shamisen and other body playing dance

surround him, like this Fete-Day Dance to be continue through the summer night and it is blest playing for only countly pupils at pressent.

By this point, the eyes and wits of the transcriber seem to be dancing crab-wise after these queer intimations, and probably the reader also feels a little dizzy.

(1926)

PART THREE

ENGLAND

BELLS ON THE BREEZE

A KINDLY tramp, with flaming beard, met me at the far end of the lane as I was coming through the kissing-gate, carrying a yellow flag-flower and a white water-lily (already strangely disenchanted). I was also eating a green apple, my first of the season. He spoke: 'Don't eat that, Jack; it'll give you the Guts'-Ache'. My ears tingled; I blushed — my only answer; what could I say? 'Guts'; what language! It was as though the blue sky had turned rusty. In one mono-syllable, the scaly depravity of the human spirit seemed revealed to me. I hurried from the scene of slaughtered innocence; and the queer thing is that when I pass that scene this afternoon on the way to our village cricket, my mind will feel a trifle uneasy, Edenless. . . .

But that first cricket match went off without a shadow. I was in the village choir from the earliest possible age, not so much for musical as for moral and cautionary reasons; and every year the boys of the great houses of our parish, released from their preparatory schools, challenged the choir to a cricket match. I found myself, by one means or another, included in the choir team, and at last my turn (No. 11) came to go in. At the other end was 'Froggy', the youth who had been beating the ball in all directions. I was received with compassion; the bowlers treated me to lobs. This went on until they were tired of it, and they began 'hurling them down'. I survived that just long enough for 'Froggy' to reach his century; I had nineteen, and then observed that my stumps were at angles. How joyfully I walked beside 'Froggy' towards the pavilion, in that golden sunshine, tasting honour and glory! Now I come to think of it, the applause would have been for the youth whose whizzing hits had gathered a hundred runs; but I did not at the time go into the niceties of the case — we were a triumphant pair of batsmen.

Practice for such crises as that had been carried on with a rag ball, at making which Mrs. C., of Church Cottages, was wonderfully quick and expert; but still, we pined for something superior, something which would fly farther. Butler's shop sold fine rubber balls, price twopence; and one day the curate's wife, a lady of a primrose-like complexion, whose smile was to me angelical, gave me some notes to deliver here and there and twopence for doing so. Scrambling through my round, I darted to Church Cottages and showed A.C. the divinely provided twopence. At once he rose and indicated the urgency of visiting Butler's shop. But, just as we reached the foot of the church steps, we saw before us an old woman, a stranger, and obviously a beggar; and she saw twopence in my hand. 'Is that your mother's money?' she said. I said: 'No'; and then, remembering a story of a good, much respected boy I had found in a book given me by the effusive Miss K., I added: 'You are poor; will you have this penny?' (There *were* penny balls.) The old witch took it and remarked: 'I must buy myself a bit of bread, so give me the other one too.' I paled, but did. The horror and contempt of A.C. at these proceedings haunt me still at the bottom of the church steps; and charity has never seemed to me quite as good an angel as she might have done.

The notion of angels possessed me oddly in those days. One day a large roundabout was performing in the club meadow. I was all for it; but, while I was contemplating the galloping steeds ('Not half so good as Penfold's,' put in A.C.), I was beautifully diverted. Above them, round the revolving canopy, there ran a series of paintings of — angels, not ineffectual ones either. One of the pictures showed a frightful chasm between two indigo mountains, over which as a bridge lay a fallen pine. A small boy with a bundle in his hand was walking across this perilous bridge. But behind him, with hands on his shoulders, was a tall pink and silver angel. There was no doubt the lucky boy would get across. But was this painting correct? I felt indeed that angels were available; clouds at sunset were very nearly angels; but in some way the actual appearance did not happen. This visionary passion waned into something tolerably prosaic — a theory of prayer. I communicated it with success to my brother G. When we went to the wicket, we silently petitioned the Deity to give us a few runs. Throwing in our lines at Two Bridges or Mill Place, we prayed for a roach or two, possibly a chub. So seldom did advantage come of these supplications that in the end a disgraceful formula was evolved. If Heaven granted the boon, we undertook not to break into the plantation on the way home; if not, we were free, and willing, to take our cherries or apples. I am not sure whether even this was the final state of that theory of prayer.

Fortunate are those children whose homes are near some pleasant half-river, half-brook; and, from my early luck, I can always live delightfully in George Peele's verse on the bower:

Seated in hearing of a hundred streams.

It needed no classical poetry then for us to personify our many rivulets; they, like the dogs, the butterflies, the birds of the village, 'had a purpose, and their eyes were bright with it', where they hurried round the black-green stones and twinkled over sand and mother-of-pearl shells. Now they were just one being, now a host of fairy-like creations. The Beult was not itself, though, where it formed the sombre pool under Chevency sluice-gate. To my feeling, it merely passed through that prodigious pit, and was glad when it was by. Of the depth, the inhabitants of that pool, we were zealous imaginatives. Under frosty stars, the mill-keeper said to my friend, his son, as the roar of waters grew on our hearing over the low ground, that the pool in flood would be 60 feet deep. The pool in summer noon revealed big steely-blue chub; we could see their designed scales through the crystal shell of the surface; and our imagination mingled with realities. For, at such a time, Will B. pulled out a bream, and what a bream he looked to us! 'Mother!' shouted he, and she came hurrying from putting out her linen on the palings of the cottage garden. She looked at the fish dangling from his important hand, and mildly disagreed with his assertions — 'No, not three pounds, Billy; five or six ounces'. When we considered the bream again, he *did* seem to be nearer her account of his size; but there were still others in the pool which would one day answer all our fancy, and even convince her. The day has nearly receded beyond my sense, but still there is something about that pool which does not let me peep at it through the hazels without stirrings of mystery and wonder.

(1931)

MISS WARBLE

You cannot fail to pass the shop if you stay in the town for any length of time. You may not perhaps notice it — or you may have occasion to go in for a supply of cigarettes. It is probable that there are none in stock of any brand known to you, but your time will not have been wasted; you will have seen in the flesh that rare original the proprietress, the one-time comedienne, Miss Warble.

At least, she always claims to have been a comedienne, though she hints at nerves as preventing her from playing any principal parts. Let not Detraction set her down a dresser. Public merriment may owe little to her, but in private she earns many a laugh of which she knows nothing.

Almost the half-century has she lived in the frowsy house beside the shabby high-street. For her, time stopped twenty years ago (by our reckoning). Her pale cast of thought has sicklied her outward appearance, which is something spectral. A few raven ringlets overhang her shrunk, tallowy countenance, with her muzzy eyes and detachable teeth. On state occasions she reinforces the sparse hair with a superfine switch. Her raiment nearly always advertises the charms of black bombasine. A curious jewellery distinguishes her; there is no forgetting her two-storied jet ear-rings, with their views of Queen Victoria and Brighton Chain Pier implanted, nor her imitation coral beads strung on a bootlace round her neck. She has apparently no relations, albeit she addresses an old rascal whom she overpays to sweep the shop as Dad, and similarly an old female rascal who pretends to char for her as Mum. 'Her Babies,' a phrase which might mislead, are feathered or furred. There are the 'Belgian Bird', a red and black minim which she purchased at some incredible price; the songless canary; and in special an unutterably stupid parrot — 'Mother's Boy' — who gogglingly recipro-cates her intense affection. Mother's Boy diets mainly on potatoes previously soaked in Mother's tea. Nor are quadrupeds absent. The original Dr. Nikola's cat glides in and out, and the small terrier 'Boom-de-ay', who has almost forgotten what fresh air felt like, pines in dismal luxury within. Miss Warble, too, has extended the hospitality of the wash-house to a homeless tabby, who sometimes shares the odorous foods of Boom-de-ay.

Friends who often call in for tobacco are sometimes invited into the odd room behind the shop for a social half-hour. It is a glaucous, uncanny place, crammed with mahogany and horsehair, antimacassars, mirrors and pots of plants: the walls are quite hidden in pictures of extinct queens of the footlights, dominated by the arresting enlargements of the 1880 Miss

Warble in riding costume, and in evening dress. Momently the sense of drugget curtains, ancient needlework, cat and bird odours, albums, scrap-books, china flower-girls and spilled birdseed grows more oppressive. *The Ferryman's Daughter* and *Chambers's Journal* for 1872 afford small relief. It may be that Miss Warble is in stagey mood. At such times she thrums a devastating and agitated noise on her one-stringed fiddle while in creaking contralto she 'Wishes she was Single Again'; or at the piano, with interludes of knuckle-knocking on the lid, presents 'Drums and Fifes'; or again, with one action per line, in tones of hoarse terror, declaims 'Behind the Veil'. Praise or blame from those present passes her like the idle wind. They are not her audience: she has been playing to an entranced multitude — of ghosts.

These illusions are perhaps more convincing to her through the soothing influence of other spirits. Even under the counter in the shop, among the tags, string-ends, scissors and boxes, she keeps the constant refresher. Perhaps that is the cause of her attacks of benevolence, in which she runs into the street and dispenses grey-headed collections of valentines, picture-cards and the like to passing children. Apart from this sort of nourishment, she is understood to live on rock cakes.

Miss Warble has long delighted to forecast, with a wealth of wormy circumstances, the details of her death-bed and sepulchre. She fondly ponders shroud, hearse and ridgestone, or sometimes descends to the gentility of a vault. It is doubtful, however, whether she will ever actually come to these conclusions. An eerie metamorphosis seems to have settled on her and her waxen menage, long since — a spell such as once eternized the fabled Tithonus. She suggests a ghost and ghostly immortality. The Last Man will presently call on her for his last ounce of tobacco and, in the petrified parlour behind the shop, among the dusty playbills and autographed photos of a forgotten age, be permitted to admire her miniature china piano, her ormolu timepiece in its glass mausoleum, her family of assorted pets, and her raucous impersonations of the extinct figurantes of Victorian music halls.

(1919)

THE ENGLISH COUNTRYSIDE

'MY brother's Cow,' wrote Gilbert White in his journal, 'when there is no extraordinary call for cream, produces three pounds of butter each week. The footman churns the butter over night, and puts it in water. In the morning one of my nieces beats it and makes it up and prints it'. When the excellent Edward Jesse in 1834 printed this fifty-year-old entry among his 'Gleanings', he could not repress an exclamatory *Tempora mutantur*. Since those days, our walks in our country places, our observations on village and farm aspects, are apt to resolve themselves into a sustained elegy, *Tempora mutantur*. In many districts, we have perhaps ceased altogether to seek for bucolic effects, and the apparition of a milkmaid or a 'smock-frocked boor' flail in hand would be something against nature. Change has worked with rapidity in the England that used to be so busy with harvests, corn-markets, the last load and the mill-wheel. Instead of going into the country for an adventure in primitive and pretty encounters, and a peep at an abundant round of skilful practical doings, from the wagon-shed to the wood-riding, we more and more assume the character of connoisseurs in beauty of scenery and of architecture. 'A pleasing circumstance' (to quote White's note-book again), 'mixed with some degree of regret.'

154

There are those still, such as the author of the *Corduroy* trilogy, who in their genuine chronicles of the farmer's world during these years assure us that many corners of the country retain their simplicities, their personalities, their earth-secrets, and almost their Sunday congregations. They nearly persuade us that the country has still its peasantry. From their natural and experienced narrations we rise and take the road rejoicing that there are still countrymen, powerful or poverty-stricken, who could show Virgil a thing or two about hogs and horses, and keeping a farm like a garden. We shall be rewarded from time to time by meeting a shepherd and his dog, where the wethers' bells make the breeze musical; or by passing a few hours where the cowman placidly riding his bicycle to his allotment is followed by his faithful servant the sow; or by hearing long songs about emigration and Victoria, Great and Good from the black benches of the 'Crooked Chimney' parlour. Will the little huntsman be induced to attempt 'John Peel' this evening, a song which he has yet to learn is known to his countrymen generally?

The surfaces of the countryside inevitably display your *tempora mutantur* in a conspicuous violence, but beneath them remains, even in the less promising surroundings, a deal of country community and integrity. There is a village I know which, through the influences of the War, of education, of the motor in all its forms, of broadcasting, of social modifications, of business combinations and the rest, frequently appears to be — not the same village. Half the hop-oasts whose conical white-fingered cowls used to shine above the trees on a blue sky like sailing-ships on summer lagoons are gone or going; the streams, which formerly were kept so full and clear for water supply, with their little hatches and tumbling-bays, are scarcely now worth walking along; you hardly know your neighbours, who seem to live as much elsewhere as in the parish, for work or play; the baker's vans are superseded by hasty visiting cars, and so it is with the other roundsmen and their cheerful word with every cottage for miles. Such signs, some of many, seem like an epitaph; but when I find myself thinking that way, it is time to pay a call on Old Sid. He will be, this evening, in his kitchen, heated like a bakehouse (he was a baker for about thirty-five years); he will push his spectacles back to take a good, grandfather-clock look at his visitor, and then, as his hand-coloured pack of cards begins to circulate, he will speak of all he has done, and seen, and heard around the village since we last met. What with hop-picking, cow-keeping, apple-gathering, faggotting and fetching and carrying he has been as busy as a bee; and as his talk thrives, the scene of village community and of rural affairs awakens in the listener almost as fresh and copious as it ever did. He too laments; not so much for the fiddle-playing in the church for which his father was famous; not for this particular tree gone,

156

or that old character extinct; but in a broad view, for a relationship of various talents and masteries, and courteous differences, which composed a serene, just kind of life. The spirit of our village may be declining and doomed, but in such a man (who tells youth what it should do, and is seldom resented) it fights finely for survival.

In matters of landscape and traditional 'picturesques', in whatever affects the common right of natural beauty and spiritual delights conceived by one 'forth issuing on a summer's morn', the crisis has arrived in our time, and there is a sort of civil war. To particularize here the characteristics of those who deface the land, and impoverish the sense and sensibility of the race, is unnecessary; nor may I, though tempted, make this an opportunity for describing the enterprise, imagination and generosity which have counter-attacked ruination. Civil wars in English history have not meant universal bewilderment or even disturbance, and it is no slur upon the protectors of our scenery and countryside to remark that there is a great area of the kingdom lying, and likely to remain lying, beyond the battle. Some is of a character too great and powerful to be disturbed — dramatic or epic in mass, extent and shape. It is not that:

'We do it wrong, being so majestical,
To offer it the show of violence,'

we cannot do so much if we would, the total impression being eternal. Of the other sort of English scene, where instead of moor, mountain, and cliff, we have the fine consonances of church spire and poplar and meadow path, the danger is active; yet it is seen to operate within certain limits. London, and the huge towns of the North and the Midlands, are able to crush with final force mile after mile of orchard and coppice, and to transform honest village streets into meretricious, avaricious exhibitions; but there persists a perfect freedom beyond these bombardments from the Wens (as prophetic Cobbett called them). To sum up most areas, we may still take our way without perturbation in a region where, such afternoons as these, we shall see the scarlet coats of the huntsmen, and the gay pack streaming down the grassy hollows past the church and the hall, the furze, the fern, the gilt-leaved beechwood and the sedge-embattled lake — and the question of *tempora mutantur* becomes suddenly very uncertain. The fox, if we are concerned about his part in this coloured canvas, knows his business as well as his ancestors, and apart from such interruptions can still testify (among friends) that the countryside continues to exist.

(1932)

THE LOST LEADER

HAVING achieved the full age of fourteen, he looked
the whole world in the face and rudely announced his
opinions of it. From a remote date he had eschewed
the educational way in which his father (who had the
village school) had illusions of training him: the books
of politer information on which his brothers battened
were beneath his contempt: and his schooldays had
been chequered by frequent fisticuffs in which his
betters sometimes fared worst. It was with no symptom
of regret that he clumped tyrannically forth from the
school porch for the last time and assumed the
ensemble of Dignified Labour, the Practical Man.
Not that he had before allowed the least blade of
grass to grow beneath his steel-shod feet. Only a
Bowley could ascertain his earliest paid activities.
Latterly he had not been even for a day short of ready
money, or goods in lieu; so arduous he was in assisting
local gardeners or the bright spirits in the bakehouse,
in trading his bantams, or in delivering telegrams (with
the aid of his highly-trained goat and its wallet).
And so independent had he become that he could
afford to rebuke the reverend vicar and sever his
connection with the parish choir, whence he had
drawn some slight emolument (not slight to other
children) every quarter.

159

But it was the War which brought him to the pinnacle of his glory. From the very outset, or earlier, he had marked it for his own. In fact, with almost inspired and certainly imaginative utterance, he was in advance of the rest of Dumpstead to notice it. Blundering in one quiet evening he horrified the family with his news of fleets racing up the Channel and Russian steam-rollers leaving for Berlin. With alarming insight he presaged that the Russian army command intended to march clean through Germany and (by way of overtime) invade the shores of Britain. He spoke, or rather bawled, with the air of one divinely informed — red, sniffing and bolt-eyed.

His position was now (for he preferred the practical to the metaphysical) that of butcher's boy. Functioning thus he daily propelled, with violent lurchings to alternate sides, a mammoth cycle laden with meat. Hero-worship for his employer and a sense of responsibility made him deaf to all sarcasms. The War had lasted some seven days when he presented himself at the recruiting office of Stillbourn, a neighbouring townlet, as a desirable Dispatch Rider, Groom, or Field Gunner. Let imagination paint the scene of this mandrake confronting a gigantic sergeant — this skinny, undersized youth of amazing keenness, arms akimbo, head on one side to express unrivalled cunning, clad in a check cap with extraordinary peak, corduroy suit, black leggings and hobnailed clodhoppers. He was told with good humour that he

could not be enlisted. The injustice of this so vexed his
spirit that eventually (despite, or because, of his
controversial skill) he was ejected 'with yell and blow'.
The call of khaki, however, could not be silenced by
any disappointment. Within a fortnight he had
acquired a pair of puttees. Within a month he had
quitted the calling on which first Cardinal Wolsey
and second himself had shed lustre, to attach himself
unofficially to a field battery, then training at a camp
a few miles off.

For some months the paternal hearth knew him no
more. With uncommon confidence, wanted or un-
wanted, he had established himself among the
permanent camp staff. Possibly he cleaned buttons,
conveyed messages or otherwise displayed his philan-
thropic mission; his family saw him not. More
tenuous, less tangible than the Scholar Gipsy, he was
espied once or twice in passing lorries, doubtless giving
the drivers the benefit of his mechanical experience —
in a cycle shop, *aetat* 12. It was whispered, probably
on his own authority, that he was the battery mascot,
and certainly one evening his brother saw him (proud
manipulator of a swagger-cane) emerging from a
Y.M.C.A. hut with two bemused artillerymen. The
day, however, arrived on which the gunners left their
muddy haunts for yet muddier; and it proved impossible for our hero to cross the channel with them.
Shortly after midnight the Dumpstead Schoolhouse
was aroused by the old familiar paces of the Practical

Man, whose surly accents were also heard demanding the whereabouts of his supper. Next morning, after dealing out swift vengeance to the smaller children on account of the deterioration (during his absence) of his he-goat and bantams, he took a walk through the parish to acquaint himself with its latest problems. Hearing that the Pup and Rasher required a Strong Boy, he immediately bearded the landlord and spoke for himself in the highest terms. Mine host had no choice in the matter and the Strong Boy at once inspected the bar, cellarage and stabling with a view to improvements. It would hardly be just to dub him a factotum in this new chase, since he was 'never done'. His labour would have been cheap at a pound a day. The same morning saw him as the following and countless other characters: The Man with the Muck Rake; The Man for the Empties; Hercules Cleansing the Stables; The Deerslayer (mice and rats and such small deer); The Tavern Junius, and Simon the Cellarer. Never was there such a youngster. A piercing whistle accompanied all his moiling and droiling, and he developed an austere cast of countenance which caused the vicar to nickname him 'King Leer'. This clerkly jape, one suspects, caused him no pain.

He certainly shone as a war-worker. Conscious of the fact, he disclaimed all acquaintance with his coevals in the village street, and confined his conversation and interests to his grey seniors, and in special

to the keeper of the Pup and Rasher. That worthy
arrayed him (at least his mortal part) in a cardigan
waistcoat, Fred Archer breeches and buskins, and
before dinner added a baize apron; affected the oracle
in poultry, parish, war or weather disputations: was
most frequently seen (in his leisure) seated on an
inverted pail, hands on knees, gazing with unutterable
pride on his pig-pens and chicken-runs. In every
punctilio the Strong Boy copied him. Had the inn-
keeper portended rain afore elevenses? Rain afore
elevenses echoed his knave. Did this Nestor of the pots
condemn Mr. Asquith as a gurt Donkey? With similar
ironies did the Echo gird at that unconscious states-
man. Everybody for miles knew our Strong Boy, and
the Pup and Rasher throve despite the absence on
service of many pillars. In the occasional beanfeasts
there for soldiers and sweethearts the following
summer, our hero's homespun wit and dexterity with
pots of tea added distinction to the already noted
Pup and Rasher catering.

So much for his public work during 1915: now a
glance at his private life. On Sundays he took his
rest, and (always accompanied by his immortal goat)
patronized the sweetshop outside the lych-gate 'at
frequent intervals between dawn and dusk'. His
sweeping contempt for the softer sex had one weak
point. He has been disturbed in the act of inscribing
IVY on the schoolhouse gate. Ivy's parent — a
cunning fox and small farmer — he cultivated with

singular care for these reasons: The prospering of his
flame, the chance of odd work in the fruit plats
(especially strawberrying), and the Yeomanry uniform
and spurs which the proprietor mostly wore. But the
affair of the heart was not his main recreation. Little
leisure as he allowed himself, he nevertheless was one
of the most dependable patrons of the penny seats in
the one picture hall of Stillbourn. Emerging thence in
a whirl of bronchos, mustangs, and dagoes, he
generally managed to visit the fried fish shop before
its proprietor had 'got dahn to kip'. The wages paid
our hero by his admiring employer, though not
proportionate to his energy, left him goodly margins
which he speculated away in decrepit bicycles, air-
guns, and the distractions just adumbrated. It is not
presumptuous, we trust, to single out one great
occasion on which he bade dull care begone and take
his spare silver with it. The day was his holiday —
'A mark of esteem' from the publican. He ordered his
younger sisters and brothers to parade, clean, at seven
in the morning for a visit to Brighton. One of his
friends in the village having a new motor for hire, he
hired it; and the party drove off in great style to
Stillbourn Station. As the car neared the Pup and
Rasher, however, he was smitten with a sudden qualm;
and, lest the watchful landlord should note the faces
and wonder why his carriage had not been loyally
chartered, he caused the joy-seekers to duck their
heads. Arrived at Brighton, he ramped like Keats

through Chapman's Homer. For the admiration of the rest he gave a display of agility, skipping in and out among the traffic in the most entertaining style, and running races with the taxis. As if by instinct he immediately discovered the cheapest cookshop in the town, and reading out the menu (written in white capitals on the surrounding mirrors) in a loud voice, did the honours there with éclat. The automatic machines, the aquarium, and the cinemas, irradiated by his enthusiasm, added to the delights of the youthful revellers.

It would scarcely seem possible that the subject of our remarks should ever leave the Pup and Rasher, for which he had perspired so freely. The severing of their loves, notwithstanding, came to pass at the beginning of 1916, and at the instigation of his parents. Their sole objection to his potmanship, he has himself informed me, was the small prospect of advancement in that walk of life; and in consequence after a series of debates and on condition of his receiving a new bicycle, agreed to learn printing at Stillbourn. His new employers were at once parsimonious, sanctimonious and ceremonious; and expected 'Sir' and orthodoxy. The pupil in a few weeks had mastered the elements of typography, and shortly afterwards endeavoured to master the Junior Partner. There was some incident with the handle of a machine. He may have succeeded: at all events he ceased compositor, and disposed of his new cycle at an enhanced figure.

And now for a time he became the ape of the small farmer and late Yeoman already discoursed of. With Pup and Rasher brilliance he embraced the cause (of market gardening): often under the cerulean eye of Ivy herself, he hoed, he grubbed, he twinkled, he trowelled. Among the lordly cockerels themselves he strutted the proudest. The inner history of the war, retailed by the ex-yeoman after excursions to see his alleged comrades at Canterbury, this manikin was always ready to elucidate for the less informed. His appearance in a cap of B.E.F. pattern and far-sparkling spurs was but a final flare, for the family was on the point of removing to a seacoast town. The farewell scene between our hero and his he-goat (alas! only valued by the public at one shilling sterling), has not, I am told, been surpassed by anything of the sort in history.

But we must not give way to pathos, however pardonable, when so much remains to be told. Let us transfer our mental gaze with him to the great garrison town of C. Here his eye roved enchanted over a never-ending welter of khaki, blue and mandarin crimson: the proud shades of England's sea-kings must have smiled to see him drinking in the uniformed scenery in an imperialist rapture. For a few days he marched his younger brethren in single file up and down the esplanade, enforcing discipline with a small stick — his field-marshal's baton: then, having completed his survey of the place and its possibilities, he

stepped serenely into the post of canteen assistant at a
barracks scarce accessible save by row-boat. From
scraps of information casually let fall by him there is a
firm conviction that he controlled not only the canteen
but also the camp. The colonel, if ever he ventured to
inspect the canteen, cannot but have scuttled forth
keenly aware of his inferiority. Is there a man whose
misdeeds would not have prevailed against him under
the soul-searching gaze of our Marvellous Boy? The
latter, however, with the unrest connoted by genius,
shortly afterwards sought fresh worlds to conquer.
His next movements were rapid, picturesque and
original. For two days he sat at a tollgate shepherding
in ha'pence, but, disputing the rights of man with
someone, left at no notice; then, he inveigled a bargee
into taking him for an up-river voyage; made his
presence felt in the coffee-bar of another canteen:
tended the ticket-box in a back-alley cinema. His
recreations — cricket, football and other academic
pastimes were his aversions — were in character.
Chief among them was his habit of hastening with a
sack through the mists of morning to the fish market,
to bid for great weights of gurnet, mackerel and so on
at bed-rock prices. Bartering the main bulk of these,
he forced his juniors at home to assimilate the
remainder willy-nilly. He also became adept at
borrowing boats by shock tactics, to be seen immediately rowing violently up and down the sound. On
one occasion he was even so fortunate as to locate and

bring to land three floating corpses. He might perhaps have earned himself a catafalque in the Dictionary of National Biography of 2000 A.D., had he not ceased to follow the gleam and become one lost soul more. It is poignant to record the total eclipse of this bright star . . . 'prepare to shed them now'.

Once again, the daughters of Eve encompassed a man's ruin. He accepted employment as cinema operator in a small sea-port, and from that moment, despite the coruscations of the cinema, his decline began. We know little of the fair women themselves whose charms allured him to don peacock neckwear and beaver trilby *vice* the strawberry bandana and matey check cap of the good old days. It is certain that decadence stole upon him in the quest for lady's cheer, and that he, the terror of pastors and scorner of poets, in a short time carried on a correspondence touching salvation, and versified in his new loose-leaf notebook his impressions of a shipwrecked trawler. O sad no more! He last smote our dazzled but disgruntled vision, a liliaceous, grammatical being, selecting his Egyptian weed from his floriated case, and glibly referring to Bernard Shaw and Robert Bridges — or at least Arnold Bennett. How was he rarified, how become common!

It is long ago now; and I cannot collect the details of his career with the Army of the Rhine. Promotion, at all events, never consummated his decline. Why do people grow up? But sometimes I have suspected that he is one of the exceptions. To you or me, the purchase of a goat or a motor-cycle in the market would not be a lyrical impulse. But, being with him on such opportunities, I have felt that there might be a visionary gleam about them. And then, there was that midnight contest of wits with the assembling police forces of N., and the amateur detective tricks we played at B. Without him they might have been, to my subsiding romanticism, tedious and trying; with him they had the flickering brilliance of a Leadership that never can be altogether lost.

(1919, etc.)

YALDING BRIDGES

AMONG the villages of Kent, the one I have known since 1900, Yalding, enjoys one considerable distinction; within its illogical boundaries it preserves two of the ancient monuments to which State protection has been granted. These monuments, moreover, are not mere antiquities, but modern, essential workers in the life of the village; they are Twyford Bridge, and Yalding Town Bridge, which answer the needs even of the multitude of motor vehicles which pass through the place. No one who comes to see the village will miss them, particularly if there happens to be a flood at the time. Yalding would scarcely be itself were the floods to cease altogether. The Medway is here joined by two streams, the Teise and the Beult, and by several 'petty rills,' and when unusual rain or thaw act on the country, often we have found ourselves in a small, pale, gleaming inland sea.

These waters have, in their time, received poetical honours. Spenser, in his *Faerie Queene* (1596) marries the Medway to the Thames with a great display of river-fancy, and thus he dresses the bride:

Then came the Bride, the lovely *Medua* came,
Clad in a vesture of vnknowen geare,
And vncouth fashion, yet her well became;

170

That seem'd like siluer, sprinckled here and theare
With glittering spangs, that did like starres appeare,
And wau'd upon, like water Chamelot. . . .

Presently he writes:

On her two pretty handmaides did attend,
One cald the *Theise*, the other cald the *Crane*;
Which on her waited, things amisse to mend,
And both behind vpheld her spredding traine. . . .

Another illustrious Elizabethan poet composed a wedding of the Thames and Medway — Michael Drayton, in the *Polyolbion* (1622); he allows the Medway three bridesmaids —

Teise, clear *Beule* and *Len*, bear up her limber train.

To put matters more prosaically, Yalding marks the middle point of the Medway's course, and the end of that of the Teise (seventeen miles) and Beult (twenty miles).

Though the great ease with which London sends out her crowds has not improved our rivers, we may yet claim that they are beautiful. Perhaps the turning Teise is the most graceful of them, where it plays from pool to pool under its willows and hawthorn bushes, and through wilderness of hemlock and convolvulus and nettle. The Beult runs, for the most part, deeper and more sullen, and yet has its sandy and stony shallows, and forget-me-not spreading into the light

ripple. Where it joins the Medway, it is sluggish and
fenced with sedge and rush on clay banks. The
Medway itself is here so deep, and its margin so
sheer, as to have been a death to many. Above
Twyford Bridge, however, its solemn advance is
interrupted by a waterfall, and it divides into two
ways. The Old River meanders under the arches and
round a broad meadow-land, sometimes swift, sometimes slow, with crocodile-snags jutting muddily
out of dark corners. The Barge River, or Canal —
made in the reign of Charles II — takes a direct track
until it pours through Hampstead lock into the Old
River, and both flow on together towards Maidstone.
Your kingfisher keeps to the Old River.

He of course is not the only angler who has a passion
for this triangle of streams. For many years the
Anchor Inn has been a landmark for enthusiasts, and,
as most of the fishing is free, some of these have come
from a distance. Old natural historians repeat a
story or two of immense eels and pike taken in the
Medway at Yalding. Bream and roach are more
usually waited for, and the sultan-like perch may be
seen now and then with his wonderful poise by the
old timbers. The Beult also has its shoals of bream,
which, normally as contemptuous of mankind as our
Yalding stonewaller is of the off-theory, sometimes
lose their heads all at once, as nations before great
wars. Chub take a cherry now and then below the
bridges, and there are plenty of dace and bleak —

those almost winged wanderers. The present writer may mention even that he once took a trout in the Teise — on an inch of bread-crust, too; but that was before the war, and things are altered. Our waters are nowadays very tired. As soon as the hard weather goes, they are assaulted by the worse sort of anglers — those with tackle like some torture-implements of an Inquisition, and vagabond youths with a nail attached to coco-nut twine — who, not catching much, flog the unhappy water, and bombard it with the litter of the tin-can age.

But a word more of the bridges of Yalding. These are very ancient. In a pocket-guide to England published three hundred years and more ago, I find a map of Kent, and on it, few as are its details, both Twyford Bridge and the Town Bridge are clearly marked. They appear, too, in the map provided with the early editions of Camden's *Britannia*. Even at that date they must have been two hundred years old, or so. Both are of great length, and of massive stonework, with angular recesses so that foot-passengers might not be crushed against the wall by wagons of wool, or herds of cattle. From time to time small trees spring up in the crevices of the buttresses, not to mention many grasses. At Twyford, it is not yet forgotten that a ford exists as well as the bridge, and not many years since Mr. Noakes annually rode his horse through the river to maintain the right. But Twyford Bridge was always regarded with pride by the village. In 1475 John

Curch bequeathed 3s. 3d. for repairing it; in 1488
Robert Parfett also left money for the purpose, and
John Harrenden in 1509 willed that his executors
should 'sell all my tools that belongeth to my craft'
and that the money should be 'bestowed about Twyford brig'. Such bequests also benefited the other
great bridge; Thomas Brodingbury in 1474 and the
said Parfett in 1488 are recorded. Yalding Bridge
seems originally to have spanned a shallow mere,
spreading between two channels of the Beult, and re-
created even now when the river is high. Out of this,
on a mound, has stood and still stands the butcher's
shop on the bridge which is one of our main curiosities.

These two noble bridges with their round and
pointed arches, their hand-worn parapets, their con-
tinental pavements, their splendid strength defying
the winter violence of the rivers, are ours; to speak of
the others in Yalding must be an anti-climax. A strong
stone bridge crosses the Canal near the railway, opened
with some festivity about thirty years ago; it replaced
a tremulous wooden one, so steep that carters had
difficulty to make their horses reach the top. They
whipped them up a long way before the bridge began.
The Beult, a stone's throw below the old weir at
Cheveney, and where the disused bye-stream of the
mill returns to the main river, is crossed by a flat iron
bridge (another of the solid works of the early Victorians), and this with its white fence and its abutment
of brick is pleasing. Here, I once saw an angler (a

very pious man) trussing up a frog as bait, exactly in the horrible manner recommended by Izaak Walton. The alders and willows hereabouts were formerly much less harassed by the axe, and then the stream was every way richer, and a favourite haunt for persons in love, as well as boys with an eye on the gudgeon that came to the fresh, dark green and white cascade over the black stones. Those stones perhaps are the remains of an older and no doubt a famous bridge, for the locality now goes by the name of Two Bridges, and New Bridges. I suppose I liked the River Ancre between Hamel and Thiepval in the autumn of a year of holocausts because it resembled this little nook of our village. In my dreams nowadays they merge into an identity, and shells just miss the alders of Cheveney-lez-Miraumont.

(1931)

ON PRESERVATION

I AM not sure what is meant by the Preservation of Rural England in all lights. Yesterday, three of us pulled up on the side of the lane that leads to an old mill, in a happy valley — a mill that we remembered at work. In those days, there was a mill-head, a broad water and many-lilied; now there was not, the mill-wheel being at rest — only a swampy flat of charred reed-clumps, with a tarnished stream sneaking through it to the bridge and there falling, as we had seen it long ago, into the deep round pool. Some trout were still to be seen, cruising in the middle of the rippling pool, and a jack or two lay on the far clay-banks under the rising wood of birches. A tree-creeper was running up this bole and that like an automatic mouse. The ivy trailed and flickered from the bridge buttresses, and a knot of primroses there seemed rich

As golden lamps in a green night.

Here, we had come once without restraint, knowing the miller; when there was work, all was natural beauty; but now, looking towards his old house, we found that artificiality had intruded. A gentleman in a purple golfing suit had emerged from the house, which had been liberally 'done up' almost to the colour of his own strange attire, and stood suspiciously eyeing the three persons who leaned over the bridge wall gazing at an English millstream. We wondered; then we saw that, after all, he had several chicken-coops in the meadow below the mill. No doubt he was an impeccable person, leading the country life, preserving the old Elizabethan structure, and the rest; but I suddenly wished to help the miller's ghost and pull down that dead mill with its still floury machinery, that house made epicene and unlocal.

What justification was there for such a thought? Was it only sentimental? or the grimace of the banished lover? or the touch of Cromwell in one's racial in-heritance? 'I cannot bear a French metropolis', wrote Johnson, asking for the attention of the Stuffed Owl, and I am not very kind to metropolitan 'preservation of country corners'. Yet, I suppose, I should be. Half a loaf — but there comes my miller's ghost again, good old Dusty. I will try to explain to him. England is changed, since he put up his last almanac of markets on this nail (in 1907; did he lose heart a little after that?). Windmills, watermills, grammar schools, malt-ing-houses, hop-kilns, wooden bridges, woodlands, winding lanes, great estates and farm cottages, are no longer so firmly established in the order of English existence as they were for a few centuries. Either they disappear, or are converted into some part of the new machine, which, dear Dusty, enables us to spend the day in town and be at your old sluice an hour and a half after leaving Oxford Street (you remember it, and your horse-bus adventures, once in five years). True, we cannot help bringing some of *our* dust with us — but we spend money on brightening and improving your premises. Certainly, they don't look quite natural now, but then they aren't. *We* are not; we have not yet built our new Jerusalem. No, either you accept the remodelling (I said *remodelling*) of your England, or else it vanishes like a disabled mill-wheel; or, we may make a little by treating it as a museum. This way to the Lovely Prospect, Observe the Rustic Thatch. Old Smithy — an Example of the Beautiful — Teas, Haystack, 'the Favourite Object of British Painters; Note Pitchfork, combining Elegance with Utility.

On the Western Front, now, a few lengths of trench are exhibited. The tourist sees parapets, treads along duckboards. These are not the parapets and duckboards that one knew on many occasions; there was a certain intimacy in a sandbagged buttress of earth, a wooden duckboard. The new exhibits are mere concrete effigies (they would have been useless!) lacking the natural touch. When a flowering has been completed, of whatever kind, who can defeat mortality? Embalmers have not done it.

And has the flowering of Rural England, which was in part accordant with the distinct emerging and triumph of the English genius, fallen into the sere? To me, and not to me alone, there have been some

178

signs of this decay. If it is upon us, no amount of idealism, combined with practical skill, can affect the matter long. The pressure of new ideas, new aims, a new social organization, and ultimately a new type of human being will be too great. We Victorians and Edwardians instinctively recoil from this consideration. But once I listened to Mr. Rabindranath Tagore in Tokyo (which has since expanded enormously) urging upon the Japanese the charms of, and the urgent necessity to return to, village communities; and I have heard of Dame Partington, and of evolution. We have had the England we wanted, the future will have the England that it wants; and it may not be the same. Many wise judges among us agree that it ought to be as near the same as our foresight and sense of duty and beauty can bequeath. I admire the nobility of their words and their works, which already ensure that certain choice spirits in the times to come shall see, here and there, the wonderful perfections of old England in bloom. That is a mighty resolve, too, which says that we must educate the new age in an understanding of the beautiful — a fine and sweet benignity is in it; but already we know not so much (to quote Mr. de la Mare) that 'beauty vanishes, beauty passes' as that beauty is relative, and her forms are not fixed for ever. To us, the purity of the Downs, the 'chain of pearls', is everything; but others are already fashioned by the human mart into another way of seeing, another beauty. And, after all, there are discoveries; the eyes of a dog in the beam of a motor-lamp are a beauty which our old horse-brake did not give us, and night has new trees to show.

To what point have I come? Not to pessimism nor ingratitude nor any impertinent discouragement. Nothing is discouraging that is beyond man's control even if it clashes with our wishes; the force of the main stream of nature's development is not for our despair, though it involves what we feel to be cruelty and destructiveness incalculable. Meanwhile, the business of the English is to 'give beauty all her right', for many will see Rural England as their own preservation for a long time yet, and, if the real life of the countryside is doomed gradually to run dry, and the character of survival will be a little like that of first editions in glass cases, there are museums, and museums. There are some aspects, of course, of our country's beauty and dignity which will now hardly ever be endangered or made even partially inanimate; and for the rest, even my grim country enthusiasm sees that there is virtue in a compromise.

(1931)

LORD'S, JUNE 27TH, 1930

'OF course,' wrote that classical clergyman Pycroft, '*Elysium* means "Lord's," ' and though weather and cricket are fickle pleasures there were periods on the first day of the 121st Test Match between England and Australia when I felt that everyone present — we were a noble army — was of that opinion. For one thing, the day was richly beautiful in spite of omens and thunder-hints; those drifted away, and lustrous serenities came over the scene. That scene, a few minutes from the town's confusion, became a jewel in the sunshine. The field itself, with its minutely varying textures all blending into one softly glowing green-sward, was a quiet miracle; the thousands of watchers round it, above it, formed a frontier of colours, not loud nor dull, dappled with flowery reds and blues and greys; then higher in the pure sky the flags and pennons twinkled, nearer the sun, duly more brilliant and gorgeous. It was no moribund sentiment which made me think of the spacious, defined colour-prints of the past, and even peopled the ground with the names of heroes, Mynn, Felix, Wisden, Pilch. . . . Whoever they were, the cricketers completed the picture; their 'white designs' ever shifting round the basis of the spectacle — the wickets pitched in the middle — gave an illusion of a happy immortality, a perennial occupation remote from this world's foolish anthill logic, in a better country where art is all.

Enter the Australians. Enter Hobbs and — not Sutcliffe. The usual guessing ends in the murmur 'Woolley!' Wall, whose run seems to begin from the verge of the Pavilion, is a fast bowler, but Hobbs has (some years ago) rearranged his dimension of time, and the ball arrives on his bat when he chooses. However, it is not Hobbs's day; a sharp ball from Fairfax, the hands of our candid friend Oldfield behind the stumps — another man who makes time — and Hobbs has left Woolley to continue those Attic shapes which result in the ball rebounding from the railings. And Woolley does. Hammond, who comes in, seems uneasy, and his hits mainly go to the conjurors who, by telepathy with Woodfull, are always reviewing their position, and the batsman's psychology. Woolley casts a spell over the ball, and it has to be thrown in by the spectators from its appointed corners of the field. Woolley looks at it as it leaves the bowler's hand, and one almost questions why he troubles to enforce his decision with that bat — but it is all in the ceremony. At length, however, while we applaud, Grimmett comes on. It is lucky for Woolley that the plot of Grimmett and Oldfield does not instantly work. It looks as though Grimmett with his hand on the ball is a superior magician even to Woolley; and suddenly Woolley, his electricity a trifle disturbed, lodges a commonplace ball from Fairfax in the hands of Wall.

Grimmett, with his steps to the wicket, and gesture rather than swing of the arm which so fascinated Woolley, is the old cunning round-arm bowler of the village green *in excelsis*. Wild youth may hurl the ball in fury, but that is open warfare and understandable. Then appears Wisdom, eccentric, six moves ahead, secret, exploring the batsman's soul but aiming at one of the three stumps — which one? Duleepsinhji, who has begun his first innings in these Test Matches, wears down the resourcefulness of this great bowler, but Hammond, who has been very usefully employed in thumping the ball away from Australia, shows a correctness in advancing towards Grimmett's bowling that Grimmett approves. Another forward stroke, another — and the ball falls a little shorter, takes the lightning's forked track, and the wicket is broken. 105 for 3.

In these circumstances, the appearance of Hendren is scarcely enough for our peace of mind. We doubt *his* peace of mind in these final inquisitions. However, his attitude promises well; he twirls his bat and sets himself to meet anything that may emerge even from Grimmett's incantations. His pugilistic cricket for a time dominates even the fine excess of Duleepsinhji's genius. It must be almost enough to make even Hendren give up cricket when so many pithy hits end in the hands of these fieldsmen, who receive them as aristocracy might take a note from a salver. Nevertheless Hendren has made 48 runs when, dismissing a ball towards the Pavilion, he watches McCabe insist on its resting with him. Cheerful and free, Chapman joins Duleepsinhji. He may not feel as he looks, but he looks as though it was Grammar School *v.* Priory 2nd. The touch of the supernormal is to be countered. His short and energetic innings ends, and Allen, in his first Test Match, introduces the sense of strain again. He is bowled by a yorker. 239 for 6.

Once that score in such a match would have satisfied the provinces, but at present it is not very rosy. Tate is next in. He comes to look into the matter, Test Match or no Test Match. It is among friends, and he has a word with everyone in reach, while dealing with the bowling and the running between wickets, at which he discloses that his mind in the cricket field is among the most rapid. He seems inclined to let Duleepsinhji have the bowling (of which, indeed, he has not had his share for some time), but, finding that it does not happen, he resigns himself to collecting runs in turn. He hits his boundary with an air of 'Take that', and the next ball he probably hits to the boundary, too, as one unnecessarily answering a question a second time. But turn to Duleepsinhji. You had offered two to one on his century. His score is 98. He is still classifying every ball. At 98 he cuts a ball gloriously, and a fieldsman some distance off makes a long arm, and nearly catches it — but Duleepsinhji has us all standing and shouting and waving a little later. His century is India's, as well as England's. He settles again to his campaign, and after tea his score goes up rapidly, but he seldom fails to use each pause for a look at the pitch. So the tunnellers listened under the trenches for minute messages of danger.

The sun shines on Tate as his score also mounts. Tate is in this Test Match, apart from his genius for cheerfulness, as the man who can bowl eminent Australians out; but, in a spirit of entire philanthropy, he has further expressed himself by obtaining 54 runs. Then he is caught. The unexpected cautiousness of Robins, who follows, grieves the 20,000, or most of them; it causes speculations as to the English policy. Not enough runs, perhaps, the mere 350. Robins, at all events, is inharmonious; he is caught by Oldfield; and White of Somerset is in with Duleepsinhji. White, no mean batsman, gives us further proof of the impossibility of hitting a ball in any other direction than that of an Australian pair of hands; Duleepsinhji reiterates the possibility, and as soon as Grimmett releases his latest firework he is down the pitch to it. A series of perfect drives, bringing his score to 173, though the figure seems irrelevant and the scoreboard for once unheeded, is offered to our belief. We have almost forgotten the formidable emanation of Grimmett; but it is as though, when Duleepsinhji's last great shot has been caught in the distance by Bradman off Grimmett, the batsman saluted that quality in the bowler which he has been governing most of the day. A handshake from Australia's captain as Duleepsinhji leaves the

wicket in the midst of the hallelujahs of all these wit-
nesses completes the most dramatic work, perhaps,
ever seen on the cricket field. (If that is not true in one
way, it is in the main.)

There is only one difficulty. The time left is too
short for Australia to begin batting, and England (387
for 9) must finish the innings. This painful duty of
anti-climax falls on White and Duckworth. With
great reasonableness, they perceive that they may send
us away in comfort by achieving a minor objective —
the total of 400. The odds are against them. The
bowlers know all about them. They are not Duleep-
sinhjis. But Duckworth reawakens the roar with a
fierce boundary, White lays on to Grimmett and does
the same; the pair amuse themselves and astonish us
with slogging and run-stealing, and they are still at it
when the close comes, and an umpire pulls out a
stump and flings it to the ground as though to say
that Elysium is, like all our works and holidays, a tale
that is told.

That was the first day, and even now, after the
astounding sequel, it shines with its own tints of light.
Who would have had it much altered? Suppose that
Chapman had detected the compact of Australia with
the gods of cricket to come off all together, and produce nearly 600 runs for two wickets, and declare with
729 for 6 hanging over the English hope; would we
have wished that first chapter to be less hither and

thither? Was it not romantically just and Hamlet-like in Duleepsinhji to bring his innings to an end when he did, and with that gay, generous exhibition? We lamented at the time the apparent uneasiness of Hobbs, the reason rather than the mode of his exit; the second innings almost made up for that, in a way, so far as the feelings are concerned, by the decisive second in which Grimmett bowled him. That defeat of one world's master by another was the last word; the ball was fantastically made to concentrate all that 'sort of riddling terms' which, whenever Grimmett begins his dance, assail the spirit of the batsman, and create a necessity that something intense must pass before our eyes.

(1930)

LIFE ABOARD A 'TRAMP'

IT was the depth of winter when I left East Anglia's leaden low sky and steely frozen watermeadows behind, to discover what a sailor's life is in these days; the icy blue water of the docks, the frosty lights, the serpentine reflections in the swilling tide all made me shiver as I stood for the first time on the deck of a 'tramp'. The coal trucks tilted their tons down the tip into the hold, filling the dusk with grit and grime, to the tune of a kind of gnashing thunder; the third mate with his coat collar turned up stamped his feet and tried to be sociable; but I felt confident that once away from this northern winter there would be something of the Yeo-ho-ho spirit about.

When several months later the ship was tied up in the same docks on a serene evening, with gentle stars in a silver-green sky, the pleasure of return was mingled with a natural remorse at parting with a type of men who, with little reward, recognition, or share in the amenities of life, still keep up a distinctive heartiness.

Memory, the fond deceiver, has never been able to persuade me that the merchant seaman is to be envied, or that the sea is one glorious adventure, nor did my shipmates ever argue to such purpose. They had their moments, indeed, of depression — not many, considering the routine and discomfort of their job. I felt somewhat ashamed, as I said good-bye to them, that I was returning to comparative luxury, and that I should no longer share their occasional escapes and relaxations. How finely they pretended to themselves that they were 'having a good time' in the fusty area of sailor-town! No idealists could have more freely passed a bottle of beer round as though there was an endless supply where that came from. It was the only one affordable! No patriots in Whitehall ever ranked the British lion higher than these did as they stalked in their reach-me-downs through the splendid avenues and squares where southern wealth and power rose in magnificent buildings and glided by in numberless glossy cars.

I think I see them still, hard up but clubbing together enough for an evening prowl through some unlovely dockland, where the ceaseless insects hiss among the dusty, wiry weeds by the long cracked pavements, and around the myriad street-lamps which are set between tramp ships and the theatres and restaurants of graced citizens. Their loud unintelligible questions ('Hullo, Mister, where's the London Bar from here?'), to natives innocent of any English, their discussions of the English Football Association, the United States Shipping Board, the next charter-party, ring out on the ear of fancy. They applaud the apprentices boxing away at the Mission, fall in love with the local beauties who come there to lend a hand and join the dance, decide three nights later that their case is hopeless, and scribble a letter to Miss Z. (now enthroned again) at some seaport in the British Isles. That done, they spend the last evening before the ship is to leave in the gaudy dance-hall packed with wild-looking 'Dagoes', and as they return thence cannot help calling at the London Bar to instruct the sleepless waiter in card tricks. And, before the boat moves, they will once more be on the wharf alongside taking hasty tremendous kicks in the blazing sun at the ship's sole football, and rescuing it if necessary by swimming for it through the greasy fetid water streaming seaward round the chains and dolphins and hulls.

That, of course, is not all that going ashore seemed to me to yield the sailor, but some such dreary conditions must always be his. Tin-Town clusters round his ship, and he is not always equal to the prices of the more distant and representative streets. It is easy to understand the old hand who says he is never happy until he is clear away at sea again. Out there, it is rather business than romance which concerns him, but he has his aspirations and his pleasures. Books were read hard, and roundly criticized, aboard us; there was no shame in a taste for serious subjects. Moreover, I used to find the third mate composing short stories of the most piratical fury, and declaring that he had something more than a dream of a mystery ship to sail the South Seas and provide him with a

steady income ever after; meanwhile his literary experiments gave mild offence to the second mate, who
had already some recognition aboard as a writer, and
who now issued a magazine. His watch below was
sacredly spent in writing and re-writing this production, and he had to stand to do it all, owing to the
state of his cabin. When this journal, *The Moralist*,
was published, all was glory and even the bos'n, who
had been ill, was seen sitting aft in roars of laughter.
He was in the paper as chief conductor of the 'Chain
Lightning Gang'. I think the cook was not so happy
over this publication, for professional reasons; he had
not been invited to contribute his drawings, a number
of which, in fierce-coloured chalks, were stored under
his bunk. He asked me to get him a post on *The Times*
in London, and unquestionably his pancakes would
have satisfied the most exacting editor.

Then, too, there were some hours which for simple
happiness can scarcely be eclipsed, and to all appearances my old friends were aware of them; midnight
hours when the dark sea lay peaceful, and the gush
of shining foam around the bows alone broke the
silence; moments when feathery blue traces on the
horizon grew into great islands with gleaming sum-
mits and terraces of forest and cultivation, destined
to be a long while sunlit in memory. The first mate, a
magnificent character, might open his conversation
with me, as he began his starlit watch, with dry
questions on the amount of romance I had been able

to find in actual sea life, but it was not long before he would give proof that he himself could find all that it contained. He would recall and live over again all the curious, dangerous, amusing or surprising passages of his career, pausing only to answer the look-out's call or to flash back replies to passing vessels; and for a time the inevitable years of absence from home, which he felt deeply, must have seemed as of no serious weight against the rich characters, situations and scenery glowing through the smoke of his blissful tobacco. When he had left the bridge, his successors would regale themselves and me with similar seafaring stories altogether amounting to a poetical tribute to a life which they sometimes described in very different fashion, when the cinders were flying, the cargo shifting and the 'salt junk' appeared peculiarly sinister.

(1926)

PART FOUR

THE WORLD OF BOOKS

SHAKESPEARE'S SIGNIFICANCES

A Paper read before the Shakespeare Association

SOME years ago, when I was for one voyage officially signed as purser to a ship carrying a quantity of coal-dust to South America, I had the pleasure of long literary conversations with the captain, who was a man of considerable reading. In the natural course we made our way by Conan Doyle and even *The Light of Asia* by Sir Edwin Arnold to the verges of Shakespeare. It happened that the third mate and I were both devoted to certain passages in the great tragedies, and kept up conversations largely in Shakespearean tags such as 'Help! Help . . . What kind of help?' But the captain, with his steady movement of mind and body, was not so handy with the apparent implements of Shakespeare's appeal to the gallery. He said: 'I must say I haven't yet made much of Shakespeare. I am waiting. Older captains tell me that you can't read Shakespeare until after you've turned forty.'

That remark has haunted me ever since I left him with his chart and his cigar, and although now, if I were obeying its advice exactly, I should not be qualified to stand here and read my essay at all, yet it is the endeavour to recognize why such men of experience saw Shakespeare so, that has induced me to

make my footnotes to some of the plays. I take it that
the character of British sea-captains is essentially a
resolution to understand a subject in all its bearings,
the fruit of actual education at first hand in the ways
of ships, the ways of men, and perhaps it would be
safe to add the ways of women. They, more than most
men, acquire the sense of the deeps of sea, of heaven,
of the human heart; they are accustomed to reading
the complex in the simple. A cloud no bigger than a
man's hand, a new note in the wind, an allusion over
the salt junk, and they are aware of 'a number of
things'. That sense of concealed but powerful meanings, in hints which almost pass too rapidly for observation, and which must be won, as Melville says,
out of the abysses above and underneath, is the
second nature without which my old captain was unwilling to take command of his Shakespeare. He
realized well, in his particular universe, the practical
meaning, the ideal beauty, the traditional fascination,
the intellectual importance, the emotional chances
combined in one instant; and felt that in the Shakespearean universe there is a similar accumulation of
effects, and words and phrases that operate at similar
planes of significance.

Cryptography has long since taken up her abode at
a spiritual Stratford or St. Albans, and though the
direction and temper of most of the consequent investigations have been ludicrous, there is a sense in
which all critics of Shakespeare must be crypto-

graphers. 'A sort of riddling terms' is found in Sophocles; the short and unadorned dialogue there vibrates with additional tragic purposes; no wonder then if Shakespeare, in a country full of proverb, metaphor, parable and pun, is supremely skilful in conducting his characters to their destiny by means of oracular and laconic utterances. For stage presentation, it is very probable that only the external and immediate reference of these needs to be grasped. Upon my submitting some instances of what I take to be the Shakespearean sublimation of the pun, a friend of the highest judgment in poetical mysteries observed, 'Very well; but according to your theory Shakespeare's audiences would have to be all Shakespeares.' Ultimately, it might be so; but for the transitions and logic of the moment, not so. In the cinematograph we have a scarcely surpassable case of sheer surface and rapid narrative supplying all that 'the public wants' on the spur of the moment. But even there, what King Lear calls a 'darker purpose' is the secret of continued liking and demand. It is on this account that Chaplin, the Elizabethan of the films, is the only creator of works that can be seen again and again with pleasure. In story and situation the films with which he has captured the world and held it for ten years are swift enough, various enough to satisfy the least thoughtful. But he never fails to include some deeper theme or characteristic which repays more painful thinking. The fight for the tramp on the highway of human society has sustained his work first and last; and hardly a gesture escapes him without strong emotional reason. Consider, for instance, the quiet ending of his play *The Circus*. The wanderer, who entered a world in which romance and even money came his way, and who has left it again as lonely and possessionless as when he began, sits over the ashes; plays with a relic, with *the* relic of the whole episode; crumples it up and casts it from him, and then walks with his pathetic comic peculiarity out of view. But, as he goes, one swift glance right and left, one lively skipping step, tell us that he is master of himself. It is morning, it is freedom, and in that glance we have the spirit of 'fresh fields and pastures new'. Napoleon, or Charlie?

Of this quality, and of unique degree, are the significant gestures of Shakespeare, and without pretending to offer very much that is not already extant somewhere in the commentators, or perfectly well apprehended by every good reader of Shakespeare, I shall now attempt to produce a series of examples of his myriad-mindedness from a play in which he delineates one of his most perplexing subjects. That play is *King Lear*. I do not know that it can be called a study of insanity. It conforms well to Talfourd's account of the insanity of Mary Lamb, with her peculiar imaginative *sense* in apparent chaos. It is rather a revelation of the sanity, or inevitable sequence, underlying and co-ordinating what superficially seems incoherence. And, since the play of character, incident and feeling is subtle, attention must be subtle also, even though the course of our curious considerings may make us run the risk of being styled cryptographers with a difference. I begin by noticing the way in which Shakespeare invites us to watch the similarities in initials of tragedy, or the contrasts in things which have the marks of similarity. We have heard Cordelia reply to her father, 'Nothing, my lord.' It is honesty's voice, and it sounds the call for Lear's disaster. Lear plays on the word. In the end of the scene, he grimly answers Burgundy's proposal to accept Cordelia with a dowry. 'Nothing: I have sworn: I am firm.' Already it is a danger-signal. We come presently to the menace of a secondary tragedy, when Edmund is plotting against Edgar. Again, this word: dishonesty's voice:

GLO What paper were you reading?
EDM Nothing, my lord.

And Gloucester, like Lear, plays on the word which sets his misery, if he knew it, in motion.

There is a development of pathos akin to this in the high words between Kent and Lear at the beginning, and their echoes in Gloucester's courtyard. 'See better, Lear,' said Kent at the outset, but the answer is, 'Now by Apollo', and that oath being answered again, Lear finally seals the banishment of Kent with 'By Jupiter'. When under very different conditions

Lear finds Kent, disguised, in the stocks, another combat of opinions occurs, and concludes:

LEAR By Jupiter, I swear, no.
KENT By Juno, I swear, ay.

There is a pause here. Will the strong candour of this opposition, even to the shouting back of his oaths, remind Lear of that other occasion, and make him 'see better'?

But Lear's thought has receded to original sources, as he thinks them. It was his way from the beginning. His mind, seizing on a notion, is apt to work on that without chance of being redirected in time. Cordelia's 'Nothing' is followed by a beautiful and complete declaration, ending with emphasis:

> Sure I shall never marry like my sisters
> To love my father *all*.

Lear responds, 'But goes thy heart with *this?*' He has not heard. He means still, with 'nothing'. He himself illustrates this fatal insistency in the figure of the dragon and his prey. It becomes a dominant method in his madness to catch up some idea, whether suggested to his memory by circumstances or to his mind by the conversation he hears, and to retain it and shape other matters to it with a kind of pride. This, of course, is readily seen when 'poor Tom', himself the centre of a tragic whirlwind, comes before Lear on the heath, and Lear cannot discover any other explana-

tion of this companion of rats and rain other than that
he, too, had 'unkind daughters'. That way the summit of his madness lies, but there are other and less
dreadful aspects of his iterating to himself one particular theme.

I may choose one prolonged example of these, which
has not, so far as I can find, received close attention.
Lear, from the first, is portrayed as being a little
inclined to remember his school education. His
reply to Cordelia's unhappy 'Nothing' is exactly a
thesis of the old natural philosophers — *An Aliquid
producatur ex Nihilo?* 'Nothing will come of nothing.'
Soon after, with a reference to 'the barbarous
Scythian', he appears to have Horace in mind. He
breaks into Latin — *Hysterica passio* — when describing
his physical trouble, a 'fit of the mother'; he compares
himself to Prometheus with a vulture at his heart.
He hovers about the classical mythology and the
attributes of Jove and Apollo; and Kent appears
to glance at this pedantry when he says '*thy* gods'.
In the third act, he listens to the wild account that
poor Tom, with his blanket only to protect him, gives
of his tribulations, such as 'riding on a bay trotting-
horse over four-inched bridges'. Lear listens to this
recital of vivid wretchedness, and his mind fastens on
the case of poor Tom. Presently he refers to him as
'this philosopher', and propounds to him a question,
not merely suitable to the war of elements all round,
but familiar among the ancient philosophers. 'What

is the cause of thunder?' Even in this is involved, not only the academic interest of Lear, his notion of 'poor Tom', and the weather, but some allusion to the clash of hot and cold, of his own ardent love confronted with the marble-hearted ingratitude of his daughters. We proceed. 'Riding over four-inched bridges' and other visions raised by poor Tom's autobiography have stirred Lear's recollection of a famous passage. '*Modo* is he called and Mahu' chances to chime with that. The next title he gives poor Tom is 'learned Theban', and after a little while that is changed for 'good Athenian'. In short, fascinated by Tom's amazements, Lear is all this time contemplating the position through the first Epistle of the second book of Horace, and particularly through these lines:

Ille per extentum funem mihi posse videtur
Ire poëta, meum qui pectus inaniter angit,
Irritat, mulcet, falsis terroribus implet,
Ut magus; et modo me Thebis, modo ponit Athenis.

'My true poet, the man who seems to me to walk the whole tight-rope of his art, is the man who tortures my heart with unsubstantial things, angers, soothes, fills with false terrors like a wizard, who makes me be at Thebes one minute and the next at Athens.' So, there is a unity between the scattered eccentricities of Lear.

When this Horatian byplay is still happening in Lear's mind, Edgar chances to originate another stubborn notion.

LEAR What is your study?

EDG How to prevent the fiend, and to kill vermin.

LEAR Let me ask you one word in private.

At this point Kent intervenes, but we can guess what the question would have been. How did he kill his daughters? Duly the word 'vermin' works; and in the scene in the farmhouse later, when Lear prepares to 'arraign them straight', he addresses the *idola* of his daughters according to its significance, 'Now, you she-foxes!' Towards the close of that scene, he reverts to his caprice of quoting Horace, and orders poor Tom to find some better 'garments' — he had only a blanket: 'you will say they are Persian attire, but let them be changed.' This witty stroke is fully appreciated if we see that it plays on the last ode of Horace, Book First: *Persicos odi, puer, apparatus* — 'My boy, Persian attire and I don't agree.'

With poignant chances of recovery, no sooner discovered than destroyed, Lear passes into deeper insanity; his talk then leaps from one object to another with wilder haste; and still there is a contexture in it. He has now the additional confusion of the rumoured war with France among his principal motives. And so, when he has made his escape at Dover, and comes with his crown of weeds to the side of Gloucester and Edgar, he begins, 'No, they cannot touch me for coining'; the metaphor echoes, and he changes it into actuality, 'There's your press-money.' He is 'the king himself', preparing his army for the quarrel with France, inspecting recruits. 'That fellow handles his bow like a crow-keeper.' Again we must see not only the fantasy of Lear, but the birdboy passing over the farm. 'Look, look! a mouse'; apparently a reminiscence of the classical proverb, certainly a Falstaffian comment on a supposed recruit's usefulness, and clearly a remark brought on by his spying a fieldmouse in the corn. 'O! well flown, bird,' by no great extension of this, is his enthusiasm for falconry bursting forth as he sees the hawk drop on that mouse. We have from him a picture both of the country circumstances and his life and times. 'Give the word,' he finishes, like a sentry. 'Sweet marjoram,' says Edgar. It sounds 'aloof from the entire point'; yet Lear says 'Pass'. And with good secret reason. Sweet marjoram was accounted, according to Culpeper, a blessed remedy for diseases of the brain. Edgar was clearly a friend. Some other oblique significances in this scene have been well displayed by the eighteenth-century commentators. Gloucester, eyeless, is speaking with Lear: 'Dost thou know me?

LEAR I remember thine eyes well enough. Dost thou squiny at me? No, do thy worst, blind Cupid; I'll not love.'

The final depths of distress indicated by this disinterested jesting would be enough, but Shakespeare's mark is abundance. We are to feel, even here, that Lear is pondering the grossness of mortality; for 'blind Cupid' was the sign painted over the door of brothels. More bewildering still is the accurate inevitability which pulls Lear back from his philosophy to his mad hope, as it is explained by Johnson.

> LEAR . . . I will preach to thee: mark.
> [*He takes a hat in his hand, and turns it about.*]
> When we are born, we cry that we are come
> To this great stage of fools.
> [*He pauses, looks at the hat; admires the fashion of it.*]
>   This' a good block!
> [*That is, the mould of a felt hat. It suggests something*:]
> It were a delicate stratagem to shoe
> A troop of horse with felt; I'll put it in proof,
> And when I have stolen upon these sons-in-law,
> Then kill . . .

In this manner every circumstance is made an agent as well as an accompaniment of the chief misery; it is not safe for Lear even to look at a hat or a straw.

The country symbolism of flowers, which at length resulted in those pretty little giftbooks of the 'Language of Flowers', was known to Shakespeare, and contributed its colours to the full beauty of his plays. I imagine that wild flowers were not so remote from the Londoner's life in his day that his choosing some of them to suit a particular dramatic moment from more than one point of view would pass without appreciation. It is in *Hamlet* rather than *King Lear* that his garlanding of blooms and messages pleases his creative mind most notably; there we have the rosemary for remembrance, the pansies for thoughts, and the other bitterly sweet flowers; there, too, the 'fantastic garlands' that Ophelia has taken with her to the pool are more than the chance companions of her drowning. They are the omens and the ghosts of it. Yet in *King Lear*, too, we are to use our quickest sense and our tradition when flowers come into the tragedy. I have not at the moment the means to explore fully the association of 'all the idle weeds' that Cordelia names as making up Lear's 'crown' — already we see that they carry a meaning beyond that of mere picturesque detail of madness. They are his crown of thorns. But among them the *nettle* that throngs about graves, the *hemlock* with its fame for poison and narcotic, the sickly and usurping *darnel*, can quickly be perceived as speaking to the imagination of the spectator on the elements of Lear's affliction. The same touch, I believe, occurs in the study of Othello, where he calls Desdemona:

> Thou weed
> Who art so lovely fair and smell'st so sweet
> That the sense aches at thee.

These rural instants, in colour lovely and in purpose and association sinister, may well be illustrated from the most exact botanist among our rural poets, John Clare. In his 'Shepherd's Calendar' for the month of

May, he runs into a catalogue of the 'idle weeds' —
there is Othello's —

> Corn-poppies, that in crimson dwell,
> Called 'head-aches' from their sickly smell

and there, red and purple . . .

>   . . . fumitory too — a name
> That Superstition holds to fame.

'Rank fumiter' is the first of the items in Lear's
mockery crown that Cordelia distinguishes.

It will be forgiven me if I transcribe several more
lines from Clare's poem on 'May', although it is not
one of his happiest songs of Flora, with the object of
testing Shakespeare's significances in *King Lear*.

>   'With its eye of gold
> And scarlet-starry points of flowers,
> Pimpernel, dreading nights and showers,
> Oft called "the Shepherd's Weather-glass",
> That sleeps till suns have dried the grass,
> Then wakes, and spreads its creeping bloom
> Till clouds with threatening shadows come —
> Then close it shuts to sleep again:
> Which weeders see, and talk of rain;
> And boys, that mark them shut so soon
> Call "John that goes to bed at noon".'

Now let me revert to the play, and to the moment
when Lear in Gloucester's farmhouse is about to rest

and save his mind. The storm seems past. The Fool,
shivering in his drenched clothes, waits on his master.

L E A R Make no noise, make no noise; draw the
curtains: so, so, so. We'll go to supper i' the morning:
so, so, so.

F O O L And I'll go to bed at noon.

I do not wish to rhapsodize over these last seven words,
but they impress me with their seven suggestions.

1. They are a sort of tired ironical joke on Lear's
   late hours.
2. They make a playful complaint that the Fool
   would like a little food before going to bed.
3. There is a pun on the people's name for the
   scarlet pimpernel. The weak-bodied Fool
   with his coxcomb looks like that flower.
4. But, if so, he shuts late. Surely there has been
   storm enough during the night.
5. There will be a worse storm still; and at once.
6. It is the last time that the Fool speaks during
   the play. He presages his death, with a
   secondary meaning in the word 'bed' of
   'grave'.
7. He takes off his coxcomb for the last time to
   please his old friends the audience.

It is the chief arcanum of the Fool's difference from
others that he should combine and encipher his
meanings; he is the inspired child, the comical but

uncheatable percipient of the true and the false. 'Not altogether fool' is a reserved way, Kent's way, of describing his telepathy. Duly then we find him crying out his paradoxes and snatches of songs, and, since most of them are to achieve the ordinary reward of clowning, the laugh of the majority, their connection with the matter in chief is not profoundly masked. But, when we come to that part of the play in which the sexual ferocity and treachery of Regan and Goneril are revealed in broad day, we may look back and notice that there was one character who from the beginning knew all about the secret. This was the Fool. I will quote one of his hints on the subject.

LEAR Take heed, sirrah; the whip.

FOOL Truth's a dog must to kennel; he must be whipped out when Lady the brach may stand by the fire and stink.

I had for a long time passed this by, as being merely a figurative contrast between the fate of frankness and flattery, when a friend who knows his dogs as well as Shakespeare knew them chanced to read the passage with me, and informed me that there was a latent and unmistakable allusion in it. The persons under the discussion of the Fool and the King are Regan and Goneril. 'Brache' was a 'mannerly' Elizabethan term for she-hounds, both canine and human.

It is in their prodigious ability with cant terms that the Elizabethan dramatists eclipse all after-comers at the huge game of reporting human nature. It is in working knowledge of those cant terms, which even in their immorality have the genius of a strong and spirited race, and not the second-hand smirking pettiness of more recent impropriety, that the older exponents of Shakespeare, Beaumont and Fletcher, Massinger and the others have the advantage of the moderns. Change of manners prevents us from applying the openness of a Francis Grose to all the dark sayings even in *King Lear;* but, if we understand the aims of Shakespeare, we shall see the play better in its lights and shades. 'Anger hath a privilege,' and when the deeps of these oceanic lives are troubled, then there must be a muddy violence on the surface. Thence comes the satire and the imprecation on women from Lear. Thence too such a detail as where Kent threatens to pound Oswald into mud, and calls him 'you wagtail'. The term describes the self-confident way of Oswald, yes; but more — the wagtail will be seen at such corners as the outflow of drains; more again — it was a term given to the character of a loose woman; and that finally achieves its full meaning in the play when at last Regan challenges Oswald on his relation with Goneril. 'I, madam!'

The character of Gloucester is built up with many touches which are not all conspicuous, and which have the difficult duty of making his tragedy 'his own fault', yet none the less pathetic, and always distinctly lower than that of Lear. The jovial coarseness of his introduction of his illegitimate son to Kent appears to indicate the worse side of his earlier life. He is included in Kent's equivocation (and veiled threat):

> I have seen better faces in my time
> Than stands on any shoulder that I see
> Before me at this instant.

When he comes over the heath in the storm with his torch, the Fool's exclamation is ominous: 'Now a little fire in a wide field were like an old lecher's heart; a small spark, all the rest on's body cold. Look! here comes a walking fire'. And finally, we have to learn from Edgar that the farmhouse, which seemed so welcome a refuge for Lear, the 'dark tower', held another secret, and was grimly concerned with the making of the tragedy. The eminence of Gloucester is his conscience. He is almost grateful for his affliction:

> If I could bear it longer, and not fall
> To quarrel with your great opposeless wills,
> My snuff and loathed part of nature should
> Burn itself out.

Of Lear we have many incidental characteristics. As has been shown, he is a curious student, and even at his worst times can approach his torture with the calm of a Harvey: 'Then let them anatomize Regan, see what breeds about her heart. Is there any cause in nature that makes these hard hearts?' He is a lover

of the English scene, and even as he points to the map
he expresses it

> With shadowy forests and with champains rich'd,
> With plenteous rivers and wide-skirted meads.

He is a reader of the classics, and seems when he
mentions 'the mystery of things' to have the title of
Lucretius' poem in his system; his 'thunder-bearer'
and 'high-judging Jove' are of the old poets. In
hunting, hawking, archery, tournament, the art of
war, and even football he has quitted himself well,
and through his decline he lights up at the thought of
them. The magnificence of the English sportsman is
presented in most affectionate though smiling fashion
when, even at the culmination of his tragedy, as he
holds dead Cordelia in his arms, he catches at a
compliment to his mastery.

> LEAR I killed the slave that was a-hanging thee.
> OFFICER 'Tis true, my lords, he did.
> LEAR Did I not, fellow?
>
> > I have seen the day, with my good biting
> > falchion,
> > I would have made them skip.

'Every inch a king,' he has fallen short of perfection;
but he has never fallen short of the desire for it, and
under the punishment of fate and age and the wilderness he continues to 'have one part in his heart' that
receives whatever may make his rule more equal, his

feelings more imaginatively open to the problems of the unprivileged man. In short, Lear is, without 'daubing it further', as gifted and as generous a sovereign as ever could have the title of the King of Britain; but we must know so much without any illuminated addresses from Shakespeare.

It may be that a closer acquaintance with Shakespearean criticism would have done what my friend the sea-captain's share of it has failed to do, and kept me from botching in my way the trains of thought already dignified by the scholarship of others. I will, however, run the risk of repeating the known or the obvious, while I touch with pleasure on a facet of this play singularly bright with the originality of Shakespeare, yet composed of gleams and glances finely unstrained. As *King Lear* proceeds, much occurs to lighten the movement of the passions and allure the audience along, yet so, that the ultimate darkness must be deepened. One great instrument of this is the season and scenery. At first, this topic is unimportant; we are indoors. There have been eclipses in the sun and moon, but those can have only a chimerical concern with us. It remains good hunting weather, but the plot turns, and the year turns. When Edgar is driven out, he must

> with presented nakedness outface
> The winds and persecutions of the sky;

Siberian days, with beggars' withered arms among

withered trees and shaking 'sheepcotes and mills'.
When Lear is driven out, the green before the bloom
has yet to come; the hawthorn is merely the effigy
of bony nakedness, and rain and hurricane seem to
conspire to destroy even the seed of life in the mould.
Shelter itself is a war on humanity: 'Fathom and half,
fathom and half' shrills poor Tom from his outhouse.
But this is Nature's last paroxysm. Afterwards she
softens, and speaks

> In better phrase and matter than she did.

The human tempest, wintriness and hunger do not
follow her example. They become intenser. Gloucester
may be blinded, but he comes to the 'chalky bourn'
of Dover through fields of corn and flowers; above him
the 'shrill-gorged lark' makes music, and below the
lazy sea is murmuring, the samphire-gatherer and
fisherman are out and about. Lear may be demented,
but he too moves among the ripening fields, and pulls
flowers for his head, once unbonnetted, wherever he
likes; his eye meets the mating wren and 'small gilded
fly'. In his final love-song or hymn to Cordelia, we feel
that the sunshine is playing, and the 'gilded butterflies' are coming even through prison bars.

> As it fell upon a day
> In the merry month of May — .

The sun goes out, the butterflies vanish, 'all's cheerless,
dark, and deadly'.

SHAKESPEARE'S SIGNIFICANCES

In making these notes upon the richness, and intuitive complexity, and choral harmony of Shakespeare's significances, I have limited myself to one play, and of that I have done little more than scratch the surface, with nothing like a plough. I feel too that such a style of literal criticism as I have attempted may make me seem guilty of shallow presumptuousness, like the 'critic fly' in Thomson's Seasons, who settled on the dome of St. Paul's, and decided that the architecture of St. Paul's was very rough. But the points in *King Lear* which attracted me are not roughnesses, but unions of perfection; the mind of the dramatist is such that wherever we are perplexed we are safe in agreeing with the rustic summing up 'the mystery of things': 'It all be done for a purpose' — several purposes.

(1928)

THE IDEAL LAUREATE

THE Victorian spirit commissioned a number of men of genius to remain on the chaotic scene, and still the scene of new promise, which terminated the main effects of Victorianism; to remain there, reserved yet influential, modest yet exalted, blessing at once and tantalizing the tentative regeneration. One more of them is gone, and has surprised us by going even at the age of eighty-six. The youthfulness, even the boyishness of Robert Bridges had become so perennially clear a picture that one never opened a newspaper with the apprehension of finding his name in the obituary. Since he was so exactly and happily an Englishman, it may not be inappropriate to say that the man himself was, as seen in his old age, a triumph of the English race. Whoever set eyes on him and his easy, fearless, spirited movements, or heard his fresh, decisive conversation, must have felt that a country which produces such a veteran is fortunate. Had Shelley lived into his eightieth year, there could hardly have been a surer union of strength and beauty in his presence.

The unconquered nimbleness of body in the Laureate was not more remarkable than that spiritual and intellectual alacrity which resulted in his splendid philosophical poem and final metrical innovation. Hardy, with *The Dynasts* long established among the grandeurs, ended his work with nothing indeed of anti-climax, but with a diminuendo; Bridges, with all his variety of lyric and essay in existence, had nevertheless a late opportunity to crown his labour with an invention of ampler sway and profounder speculation. He took that opportunity. Normally those who awake to find themselves famous are young in years. Bridges changed all that.

Perhaps the Victorian spirit already suspected of irony would smile faintly at the suggestion that a Poet Laureate can be other than a famous man. Nor would one overstate the case of Robert Bridges. Yet 'The Testament of Beauty' was 'the turning-point in his career', as they say; nothing like that revelation's popularity had happened to him before. His earlier writings (beginning, to the best of my knowledge, with a book of verse in 1873) had won him something like the reputation of Landor, but still more secluded and unhurried. A faithful audience purchased the *Shorter Poems* (the third edition of the collection, dated 1891, now before me, shows that they did their best). About twenty years later there appeared what might be called a 'popular edition' of his poetical works at the Oxford University Press; among those who acquired this, I proudly remember, was the present writer. Clearly the Bridges public was growing; and the observation on the anthology lettered 'Bridges to Kipling', 'What do we want bridges to Kipling for?' seemed to belong to the Dark Ages. Mr. Asquith in a moment of inspiration chose the poet for the mantle of Tennyson, transmitted as it was through forgotten Alfred Austin. Obscurity still prevailed, and the new Laureate 'reigned a private man'. Occasionally, disapproval of the situation was expressed by a journalist; the situation remained obscure. After the War, the eminence but hardly the importance of Robert Bridges began to be observed and accepted; his poetry continued to be published and esteemed. Then, 'The Testament of Beauty' lit up the academic sculpture with which the name of the Laureate was tastefully embellished, and all eyes turned with sudden wonder towards the now significant Robert Bridges.

The office of Poet Laureate has been ridiculed, and its abolition urged, by many men who should have known better, even some Victorians. Whether the last holder left any explicit statement of his view of Laureateship, I do not know; I venture to think that none of his predecessors ever exhibited in practice a fuller or finer comprehension of the functions proper to the national poet. In the first place, Bridges displayed the dignity of poetry. Servility or opportunism, that have not one of the many mansions in that palace, found no approach to him. He continued to be the same sensitive melodist and interpreter of scene and thought as before. He was not unwilling to write on a national theme — but then, it would be also his own by nature, as, the tercentenary of Shakespeare. Then, since poetry is only one of the instruments by which the character of a nation is to be cultivated, enlightened, and directed, Bridges continually brought into action his other auxiliary gifts and studies. Those were numerous. He was intent upon (to catalogue these ideals crudely) the speech of England, how he should pronounce it, and how write it down; upon the music of England, and the improvement of voice and verse in religious services; upon the general realization of poetry, in its total influence and its minor construction; upon typography, which plays for better or worse on our daily life; upon the illumining of poetical achievements not generally known; and upon the worth, cheerfulness, aspiration, and endurance of the English people. 'The Spirit of Man' was a Laureate work, although not what a narrow conception of the Laureateship would term so; its making was poetical, and its effect in companioning us at a terrible period with a rich, distilled perfume of culture was Miltonic, 'compleat, and generous'.

But these words are not in the nature of a panegyric; for Bridges remains still with the reader as he personally regards him, a private man, to whose music each is invited without strain or demand. The *Shorter Poems*, maybe, are securest in our capricious memories; their fluting was of so silvery a touch, so charming a juncture. It is nearly the hour again to repeat his,

'Wanton with long delay the gay spring leaping
   cometh;
    The blackthorn starreth now his bough on the
     eve of May:
All day in the sweet box-tree the bee for pleasure
   hummeth,
    The cuckoo sends afloat his note on the air all
     day,'

and to seek what fancy vows to be his especial 'bower
beside the silver Thames'.

(1930)

AGAIN, WHAT IS POETRY?

I HAVE known many poets, and have been many times permitted to hear their opinions on poetry; but I do not remember that these practised artists were ever able to, or even willing to, reduce their mystery to a definition. It would have been a sort of triumph if I might have noted down from the lips of one of them some splendid aphorism summing up the laws of poetry in a manner beyond even Milton's three words, 'simple, sensuous, and impassioned'. Even details of the composition of their own poems have been scantily disclosed. On the whole, my impression is that the poets, except when they are writing poems, know nothing about poetry.

They are expected, of course, to be expert observers of their business. They receive from time to time, sent forth from Vienna, Oslo, Cincinnati or Warsaw, inquisitorial papers, which they are to fill in and return to the enthusiastic inventors. They are asked questions something like these: (*a*) What drove you to sea? (*b*) Are you a smoker and, if so, do you inhale? (*c*) Have any of your family at any time suffered from sciatica? (*d*) Do you compose more readily at one time than another? (*e*) In your opinion, would a course of psychology have altered the versification of the

221

greater poets, as, Pindar, Lermontoff, Whittier, Wilde, etc.? I do not know whether the kindly inquisitors ever extort the answers they would like, but I doubt it.

Not long ago a volume entitled *On Poetry* fell into my hands, in which were recorded the courteous attempts of some eminent poets of our time to assist seekers after truth in accordance with their instructions. Mr. Belloc had responded: 'I do not think that poetry can be defined by any other word except magic, and that is a primary idea incapable of analysis . . .' Mr. Robinson Jeffers (whose strange symphonies might be better known in England than they are) began with similar evasiveness: 'The word "poetry" is one of those abstract words covering a complex of things — like the word "beauty" — so various for different persons that the only definition I could give would be a bad one out of a dictionary . . . ' The author of *Spoon River* ended his deposition thus: 'In a word, whatever gives me the poetical effect, I call poetry — whatever in words I mean; and that is as near as I can come to a definition just now'. The author of *A Shropshire Lad* also troubled the scorers, but not for long: 'I am afraid that I can no more define poetry than a terrier can define a rat. We both recognize the object by its effect on our senses. For instance, if a line of poetry comes into my memory while I am shaving, the hair bristles on my skin, and I have to stop'. Readers of Professor Housman's Leslie Stephen Lecture will recognize this statement.

As I write these sentences, reflecting sadly how long it is since I heard one whom Sir W. Beach Thomas a day or two ago unnecessarily called 'the modern minor poet' talking into the small hours about great poems, I have round me a large number of poetry-books of all sorts, sizes and ages. Why are they here? Why is Mrs. Hemans here, near Shelley? And there are dozens of others, in comparison with whom the fair Felicia is a giantess in reputation. All these are here because they comprise for me what the answers of poets to formal inquirers on their secret do not. They are the poetry of England. In this assertion, I believe I am strictly following Housmanian instructions. Professor Housman insists that the name of poetry means something already in existence, shaped by tradition, and answering our expectations. 'If we apply the word poetry to an object which does not resemble, either in form or content, anything which has heretofore been so called, not only are we mal-treating and corrupting language, but we may be guilty of disrespect and blasphemy'.

How reactionary! But let us walk warily, for Professor Housman is that elusive, cryptic, sidelong-glancing creature, a poet. He does not deny the right of mankind to experiment; he does not bring forward instances of misdemeanours in the newest kind of writers, their pretence of making poetry by way of misplaced capital letters and iterations of mono-syllables without meaning. 'Poetry may be too mean a name for the object in question: the object, being certainly something different, may possibly be something superior'. Will this satisfy the neo-poets? A printer's error will be very unkind here. But I fear neo-poet and no-poet are the same author, according to Professor Housman's judgment.

Still, someone will say, thinking of the collection of English poetry I have mentioned, in fifty years' time your shelves would include many volumes of the new verse which at this moment appears so unrelated to all that preceded, and was called poetry. I am quite sure of it. Any collection that has value as a conspectus of our poetry will include already examples of the abnormal. I have here, for instance, two volumes called *Madmoments: or First Verseattempts by a Bornnatural*, dated 1839. The pages look peculiar, for words like 'motherslove,' 'the poetsharp', 'wealthadorers' and 'farechoing' are scattered over them. The young poet writes a preface of immense seriousness, calling the age an ass, and himself 'one who inherits the Natural Sentiments and Tastes to which he was born, still artunsullied and customfree'. However, now that one may look back through the cool light of a century, one sees this talented Oxonian as a disciple, after all, of Wordsworth, Coleridge, Shelley and Keats; and I surmise that as time goes on much of the writing which now seems wildly remote from the traditional name of poetry will be seen to have been only unconventional in surface effects.

Or will the comments of Professor Housman on what was accredited as poetry during the eighteenth century apply to the general productions of our day and the days to come? He probably intended to disturb the highly respectable body of men who have lately toiled for the honour of the eighteenth-century Muse when he delivered his lecture; and he has succeeded. To abridge his protest — he describes the characteristic verse of that age as being ingenious and soulless. These men, he argues, were brilliant — and stupid. They were a 'choir of captives singing hymns in the prison chapel', and only a few of them, who went mad, managed to break away, enjoy life and write poetry. In the transitions of Professor Housman's lively argument against the eighteenth century there are weaknesses; because Christopher Smart's editor, a kinsman who was a mild, prosaic parson, excluded the radiant 'Song to David' from Smart's *Works* on the score of its showing derangement, it is not fair to blame all the eighteenth century. But the main topic is powerful and attractive.

Can that be poetry for a time which presently ceases to be poetry? It would seem — and the eighteenth century suggests particularly — that it can be; and, although the usage of the word poetry is hereabouts a little awkward, what our recent writers have given us may well be poetry to this generation even if it would not have been to our forerunners and may not be to aftercomers. With individuals, the failure of great

P   225

works to make an appeal is nothing uncommon. Who can say that the poem which charmed him twenty years ago is certain to charm him still? Experience may have broken the former consonance, or removed the need for a certain comprehension or consolation. But this entitles no man to grow contemptuous of the light that glittered once. It may be still there; another bend in the road and it will be caught again. Or it may have been a temporary thing; but it served.

The requirements of periods change as do those of individuals; and if the present time cannot be moved by the rhythms and exhilarated by the phrases of much traditional poetry, let us willingly admit the fact. I have been asked more than once lately if I did not agree that 'sonnets were dead'. Dead!

> At the round world's imagined corners blow
> Your trumpets, Angels! and arise, arise!

However, my friends were only expressing their own condition; the world in which they had grown up had made them not merely impatient of but insensitive to the movement of octaves and sextets and the subdued chime of choice sounds. To them a fresh force of invention was necessary, and a kind of writing which should indeed not 'resemble' the old masters. I thought of them as being somewhat in the position of the steeple-jack in the picture at the top of a very collapsible lofty chimney; being afflicted with a choking fit he requests his mate to 'do or say suthing to startle me'.

We may perhaps be developing away from the poetry which Professor Housman has enriched and defended, into an age that will receive no impulse from an 'Ode to the West Wind' and no enlarged horizon from 'Intimations of Immortality'. In anticipation of this new world, the Fragmentarians (for to me their manner suggests what the orderly room looked like after the five-nine fell in the typewriter) are justifiably exploring what the old persuasion did not do. But all our meditations drive us back in the end to the question of the nature of poetry. Poetical works may come and go, but surely the central position, the function is constant? If we are hard put to it to say what poetry is, shall we again touch the hem of Professor Housman's gown, and say what it does?

There are two people in the arena. One is the poet, and the other is you or I. We will suppose both the poet and the recipient, the magician and the small boy, are ready. The poet's verse is delivered to our attention, and we are, as the saying is, moved. How? If you are like Professor Housman, the poem has a physical effect on you; like him, you may notice the skin bristling, 'a shiver down the spine', 'a constriction of the throat and a precipitation of water to the eyes', or another sensation in the pit of the stomach. You are to be envied, then, as one of the luckier mortals who are not deprived by habit and tobacco of these sensuous, primeval gifts. For my part I only hear a happy murmuring, which stirs in some recesses of the silent mind a host of delicious echoes, and it goes hard with the actual words of my poet's poem for an instant; but then I come back to his neighbourhood and to the significance of what he is uttering. I am still under his spell, but not so dizzy that I do not expect a meaning, even though it be incapable of translation into other times and other moods.

'A meaning' — the very fact of our listening to a poem is a mighty meaning. It is not so much that 'we feel that we are greater than we know', as that we acknowledge values outside those of utility and common advantage. We do this in other ways besides reading or hearing poems. We cultivate our gardens, and converse with carnations. We pass through Customs offices on our way to see unknown hills and dales, castles and cathedrals, to see and to be refreshed with a spirit we cannot name. We even watch cricket matches for something subtler than the championship table and the scoreboard. How these renewals of our inner life operate on our ordinary temper and ability it is impossible to calculate; but we know that they are valuable, and are as fountains flowing with a calm melody through all we encounter and endure.

Poetry, with its discoveries of the beautiful in familiar matters, its pictures and decisions in a few words, its singular command of 'the best words in the best order', its unexpected yet appropriate comparisons, its musical intricacy without effort, its aspiring constancy without sermonizings, has played a greater part in the history of the race than would be gathered from Professor Housman's lecture. If he had had more than one lecture to give on the subject, I have no doubt that he would have corrected the impression which his present excellent monograph leaves — the feeling that poetry is a luxury, though one of the most exquisite. That may be a question of definitions. 'Do I possess the organ by which poetry is perceived?' The majority of civilized mankind notoriously and indisputably do not'. Professor Housman adds that 'poems very seldom consist of poetry and nothing else; and pleasure can be derived also from their other ingredients'. May one not go further than 'pleasure'? Or shall poets fall in at the tail of the column headed by the astronomers and the physicists?

In the arrangement of circumstance which requires a poet and a listener for the beauty of the thing, we have noted something on behalf of the listener; what of the poet and his poem? Professor Housman speaks with authority on that side, describing the manner in which some of his poems grew in his consciousness. If the reception of poetry, with him, is largely physical so is its conception. Yet who shall go beyond his own record of a slightly drowsy afternoon walk and the sudden apparition in his mind of a verse, a stanza, presently (with luck) an entire poem? How 'easy' the first hints and notes came, with what labour and anxiety the completion was sometimes achieved, he admits, and he leaves the subject. Other poets might honour us with recollections of this kind, which seem scarce; one thinks of Coleridge's account of the composition of 'Kubla Khan', and even then one would almost join the *questionnaire* men and ask him twenty things more. Probably few men are able, after the achievement of a poem, to recall with precision the stages of its pre-natal life. On what day, under what sky, to what accompaniment of person, voice, incident, illness, crisis, landscape, reading, and the rest did the notion seem to come to the surface? How, at last, did this notion take to itself a series of cognate thoughts and allusions, finding these the dress or embodiment of words in inevitable co-relation? What were the interruptions? What was lost by those interruptions, and did the final poem equal that which hovered, a temporary phantasm, about the first phrases? It did not; but the poets will not complain of that which, though like all humanities imperfect, was their 'exceeding great reward'. They tell us very little about Poetry, but we shall not blame them, nor blame their illustrious representative when he concludes his exceptional treatise by hurrying back to his 'proper job'.

(1933)

BRINGING THEM HOME

IT is bad enough to be extant in an age when everybody almost is an 'antiquarian bookseller' and when every dreary little town is the den of those who think you only pick up a book (probably *Toplady's Sermons*, lacking pp. 161—256) because you intend to sell it to the Americans; but at least there are still some books. As I turn from cases of stone axes and arrow-heads, I reflect that I should have been collecting these in the Neolithic Age, but sadly, and with an increased air of the vanity of human wishes; for I suppose that at that date there were no books in the modern sense, and you could hardly carry home sections of caves in the autograph of such and such a stylist. I am even happy to have been born a late Victorian, and not a contemporary of the Rev. T. Frognall Dibdin and Tom Paine; true, they had wonderful advantages. First Folios in their epoch were good bread-and-butter stock. The black-letter was indifferently put forth on the barrows, as scarcely convenient for most customers in an age of desperate hurry.

But still, I am grateful for other pleasant helps to idleness among books, which could not have been mine had I not existed more or less in the Amazing Age. I cannot profess to be a genuine collector of books,

I know nothing of positive bibliography; small books I usually call octavos, and large ones quartos. Folios I seldom carry home, out of a growing sympathy with my weary body. But, so far as my preferences in size and weight are satisfied, I am a willing rescuer of books, and, when the sunbeam looks in, am inclined to smile egoistically upon my Orphanotrophium Bibliophili (they still taught dog-Latin in the Victorian sunset). I dare say nobody else would have given these books a home if I had not. It is a Janus-faced saying, but I make it obey me. Had I gone without tobacco, moreover, I might say that my books would have cost me nothing beyond pocket-money. This is a theological matter, for later excogitation.

I am grateful for the discovery of all sorts of book-coverings, but most of all, I think, for that of cloth. The howls of generations of bookbinders would ring out upon this, if my feeble emphasis could be transmitted to them, but no matter; I can refer the gesturing ghosts, armed in complete morocco, to Mr. Michael Sadleir, who the other day gave us so beautiful and so sympathetic a history of the coming of cloth. No doubt the modern situation is against me; all our books look alike to one accustomed to the variety of yesterday, but that variety is what I rejoice for, and will keep me happy as long as I have any concern with mortal bindings. My taste probably began in childhood, when we received little books of which the sides were rich and storied with their gold pictures. Izaak Walton was festooned with golden creels and rods and lines and trout and bulrushes; the old man himself, on what I think they call the back strip (so one might speak of an angel's vertebrae), stood for ever there by the hawthorn bush, baiting his hook, about to throw in again.

Who now enjoys thee credulous, all gold?

Of designed covers of this kind, an immense number was invented by the early and mid-Victorian artists. I am aware how, latterly, the essence of the thing evaporated, and many books appeared with a ridiculous thicket of meaningless gildings scrambling everywhere about their bindings. We may as well blame Germany for it; but the prettiest piece of abundant gilding round a book that I see this morning out of the period of decline is German work. You have probably seen others like it, and you may not wish to see them again; but I feel as I take up *Dichtergrüsse* (Leipzig, 1896) that I am handling perfection; the maze of green, gold, terra-cotta, fawn, blue, red-brown, of circles, arcs, twirls, stars, trellises, of rosebuds and violets and apple-blossoms, however mechanically produced, has a spirit in it all which speaks. I open the casket and at once I see in 'lichtdruck' the frontispiece I want: the girl in the orchard who had never heard of any better place to be sitting.

There was from the first a style of cloth binding which cultivated a simplicity not less delightful, for it was not a drab monotony. Examples come to hand still, even after exposure, in almost undimmed brightness. The secret, perhaps, was that the dyes used in the cloth were choice, the gilt of the inscription not less so, and, moreover, there was *some* work upon the cloth itself — it was ribbed, for instance, a bordering was impressed upon it, and it was polished. I would show as a quiet triumph a book in every way accordant with my desires — *The Letters of Rusticus on the Natural History of Godalming*, 1849, by Edward Newman, naturalist and printer. It is tall, thin (but not emaciated), and bound in bright red slightly ridged cloth, upon which is embossed at the back a series of chain-designs, and on the sides an embroidery a little more complicated. At the back, the one word RUSTICUS, so done in gold as to have just the suggestion of being rather made from twigs than from steel types, looks from the bookcase. I can only say 'Well done!' when I see human achievement so clear within its particular and well-understood limits, and I feel happy and encouraged. Or, next to it, I might have disturbed again *Rowe's Illustrated Cheltenham Guide*, a little book of about the same date, and looking as perennially fresh in its pale blue linen (again made distinct with an impressed pattern of intertwining flowers). This guide is like one of those trinkets that lie sweetly still in excritoires. It is printed in light blue ink, with engravings of houses and crescents and fashionable life in a lively black on every page; often, indeed, all the print is surrounded with the artist's garlanding, as a summer-house under sycamores. I must go to Cheltenham one of these days; there lives O., with whom the trenches themselves used to seem mere settings for celestial thoughts; there too is K., who knows his Shakespeare better than any man in England, and has still a long time before him in which to enrich criticism. But ever since the twopenny box surrendered *Rowe's Cheltenham Guide* I am half afraid to go. Too many of my fairylands have been suddenly dislimned. Even the toy-like gas works, as represented by Rowe, belonging to *my* Cheltenham, might be a dream.

Edward Moxon, the publisher who married Lamb's adopted daughter and who inherited much of Lamb's taste, must be named here in connection with the pleasures of cloth bindings, neither glaring nor dull. It would be nothing for me to praise Moxon's work in the Victorian battle of books altogether; but I await the day when someone, to complete his fame, will write a Life of him, adding to it a bibliography of his productions, severely separating the real Moxon from the rubbishy 'Popular Poets' and so on issued later by those who merely retained Moxon's name. We are still lucky enough to be able to acquire quite readily good specimens of the Moxon book, and its Quakerish binding. Unfortunately, as I suppose from lack of capital, Moxon often used a cloth which would not wear well, just as sometimes his paper was especially

liable to stain and spoil the grace of his typography.
In many forms, Moxon has shown us (who take no
notice) how to print poetry; one of his most sym-
metrical, yet unstrained, performances is the tall
volume of his own *Sonnets*, 1837. That this book is
dignified in appearance is well, for it contains many
pieces of a clear thought and a stately order, and some
to the glory of Wordsworth, Lamb and Coleridge.

I love to watch my chance of knowing more fully
a poet like this same Moxon, a man of few publications
and those circulated in a few copies; once convinced
that he had 'a thing to say', a light to lighten certain
paths, I wait for him to appear. And the odd and good
thing is that, on the whole, my scarce minor poets do
appear within my reach. During the last part of the
War you might hear the troops singing in anticipatory
demobilization moods:

> Everything comes to him who waits,
> I've got my Captain working for me now.

As a book-catcher, I find myself humming that tune;
for it is a sort of destiny that has given me many an
unusual little book. Absurd as the case is, I am scarcely
less pleased when I chance upon a *Poems by Hartley
Coleridge* than I should be if it were the Pisa edition
of *Adonis*, or one of the elder Coleridge's first editions.
What a family for the wandering bookman the
Coleridges are! I cannot pretend that I should not
like to possess so marvellous a range of Samuel Taylor

Coleridge's books, pamphlets, periodicals, leaflets
and autographs as Mr. T. J. Wise has among his other
bewildering constellations; but, the impossibility being
demonstrated, and the years rolling on, I can grow
hearty over the miscellaneous battalion of Coler-
idgeana which almost require nothing more than to
be carried home. It will be a glad day when, at last, a
copy of Dobrizhoffer's *History of the Abipones* joins the
others; why? merely because Coleridge's daughter
translated it in order to pay for her brother Derwent's
college fees. 'God love her — to think that she should
had to toil thro' five octavos of that cursed *Abbey pony*
History, and then to abridge them to three, and all
for £113.' So Lamb wrote. Or again, I congratulate
myself on distinguishing from a muddle of catalogues a
sixpenny tract (Edinburgh, 1867) called *Bibliomapia;*
well, it is a First Edition of some pugnacious remarks
by Coleridge on 'Southey's English, i.e. no English at
all'.

Assuredly we have given ourselves too much pain
and grief over the pursuit of the First Edition. Sometimes there are no two ways about it. *Endymion* — or
go without. Usually you can transplant your mind and
nearly your body to the era and the atmosphere of
your great book through some less celebrated edition.
I am not far from Charlotte Brontë's Haworth and
her London when I have the fourth edition of Mrs.
Gaskell's biography of her in my hands. At the end
are 'the reviews that meant so much'. Gibbon must

be in his quarto — in column of fours; but that is not impossible, if you forgo the pride of the First Edition. I would have had a folio *Spectator* or *Tatler* if I could; the illusion of being in the coffee-house with the wit and news of the week just from the press to read to the company would have been great; but in these octavo sets there is lurking the ghost of the country gentleman down at Exeter or so, a little too late for the fashion of the thing in London, but well able to meet his neighbours round the fire with 'some deuced clever fellows here'. Looking into one set, which certainly was not dear at sixpence, I find the signature 'John Steele' — now, there is a possible ghost worth having about the house.

The resourcefulness of those who have made books through the centuries often makes me forget the serious business of reading, and a book comes home simply because it took my eye in some way. Later on, I endeavour to square accounts by examining the author's share, and in this way I have made the acquaintance of far too many vanished hands. It is a habit to which many have fallen victims. While all the power and the skill of the literary world of to-day are expressing themselves in thunder (limited edition), they go on among the pale ruins of earlier ambition, somewhat in the fashion of Hamlet magnetically obliged to remember the ghost. Now, this is obviously reprehensible. I hereby reprehend it. I have to review, immediately, a heap of new works that have already been saluted as masterpieces, starkly original, brutally truthful, pulsing with the drama of consciousness, grasping the whole horror of the War in every sentence — and I cannot get out of it by alleging that the cloth is despicable, the label vulgar, and the print disappearing into the woolly paper. Actually, I shall be admiring a fair proportion of the book production, and I shall sympathize with the non-hero of the novel for being unable to convince Joan that they are able to live on harsh opinions of the capitalist system and the Academy.

After that, I am going out for a little while; and if you see my pockets bulging when I come back, you will remember that I said I hoped to pick up the first school edition of Wordsworth and George Darley's books on mathematics. I might even bring in something by A. L. O. E., if it has a glossy paper panel let into the cover, with a scene of a couple of goldfinches perched on a thistle.

(1930)

CHILDREN AS READERS

WE speak of books for children, and have in our minds a kind of authoritative catalogue of the reading of the young, without a sufficiently lively recollection of chance and circumstance. We like to be desultory readers ourselves, but persist in thinking of children as being readers of the select classics supplied to them. Our presents of books to young acquaintances are chosen on the score of being 'children's books', and therefore we presume that they will be read. But, when one endeavours to rescue from the ashes any fragments of one's own childhood which may yield an outline of the truth, the case is surely altered.

To speak directly, my own early recollections of what I read make me suspicious of any definite opinions on the literary affairs of youth. Like most children, while still of tender years, I imagined that I was being 'got at' by a class of glossily finished publications, handed to us by seniors who clearly took no interest in them apart from thinking that they would interest us and wean us from moral delinquencies which we had not attained to. I used to retaliate, when I had been treated with this benevolent tastelessness, by reciting 'Toll for the Brave!' at the children's party; and, having discovered from my mother that the author's name was pronounced 'Cooper', I had minor revenges too. We were fortunate children. We had very few 'children's books', but could easily lay our hands on almost every book in the house.

Our bed-room was a capital reading-room. It contained a few shelves with a curtain in front of them, on which were arranged several odds and ends of household management, including such books as were not needed below. Here stood somebody's 'Encyclopædia' of about 1860, with noble plates, especially of uncanny machinery; an anthology of religious prose and verse, which introduced the names of Toplady and Quarles; a manual of wood-carving, with an attempt of my father's to turn its precepts into practice, 'deferred' in the corner; 'What must I Do to Get Well, and How Shall I Keep So?'; 'Church Services'; a volume of plays with pictures of helmeted Romans under tents of strange device — the first play was 'The Distrest Mother'; 'Sutton's Seeds', and 'Needlework and Cutting-Out'; with a number of others. Curious as it may now appear, we never went to this library without lighting upon something to read or look at. We woke early to do that.

Under the stairs, in bundles due, the *Daily Telegraph* and *Kent Messenger* were borne to repose; but their rest was broken now and then for various causes. Sometimes the cricket of the past had to be reviewed. Or else the just ended war seemed to be a readable subject. With the newspapers would be lying grocery price-lists, or even bulky catalogues from great general stores. These, as they still do, awakened warm but unsubstantial speculations, and domestic curiosity. Why was not this or that item in use in our home? What a great day it would be when we had 'crystallized figs', or one of these rainbow-coloured football jerseys! What was 'isinglass'.

Periodicals came in now and then. *Punch* was something of a puzzle. We had never seen a flunkey, for example; and the cartoons were to us actual statements of the universe. Britannia was no abstraction. The *Fishing Gazette* had its virtues. One realized that there were anglers who used all sorts of equipment to take salmon and trout, fishes which in the illustrations looked less attractive than our minnows and gudgeon. The *Quiver*, and one or two others similar, were scanned on Sunday evenings while a lady friend, dodging our mother's imperfect piano accompaniment, scaled 'The Heavenly City' with thrills of songsterhood — and spinsterhood.

Those evenings, too, we had liberty to turn over the books which lived in comparative state — on velvet. Some were concerned with the Holy Land and voyages of Saint Paul, very neatly marked on the maps. On the whole, Gadsby's *Wanderings* upstairs was preferable with its engravings and anecdotes to these more studious and exalted writings, and Dean Farrar. Full sets of Dickens and Thackeray were present, and keen criticism of the various volumes prevailed, the criterion being the illustrations. The text, of which we heard something at almost every meal, seemed heavy, and I could never overcome a feeling of discord or indigestion in names like Peggotty and even Dombey. The *Irving Shakespeare* was not popular with us, but Scott's *Abbot* and Hood's Poems, and Longfellow's had bright pages. *Abbeys of England and Wales* and a work on the rivers of the land, though fine books, were chiefly picture-books; *British Battles* went with them, and indeed shows signs of harder wear. We studied the Western Front in good time, but without anticipation. My copy of *King Edward's Realm* and the Coronation Mug that had accompanied it, were here. What Macaulay meant by 'Essays *and Lays*' we could not feel sure. The Lays were only school poetry. We learned the titles of the *Spectator* and *Tatler*, and associated them with the period of Distrest Mothers, in brown leather and with long s's. Adam Smith's *Wealth of Nations* existed for us, as part of a satisfactory home; so did Tennyson, who however had earned our adverse vote by writing 'What Does Little Birdie Say?' and 'If You're Waking, Call Me Early'. Our poetry was in Patmore's *Children's Garland* and S. C. Hall's *Book of Ballads*.

The *Arabian Nights* were too short. We handled that book out of existence. Grimm was our fairy-historian, not Andersen. When Dickens began to be spectral, in the interludes of *Pickwick*, we rejoiced in him, and

243

asked for more. *A Yankee at the Court of King Arthur* enchanted us as a tale of wonder. We discovered the 'Apocrypha'. Presently, the Parish Library was opened after a period of disuse, and dear Miss ——, from the Old Rectory, allowed us a free choice. Finding, however, that too much sentiment occurred in this Library, I managed to obtain books from the Working Men's Club, and the Jules Verne and Rider Haggard period set in. It was a delightful season, and when I was told to try H. G. Wells, I did so with scarcely less enthusiasm. Not that Defoe, and Ballantyne, and Kingston, and the bound volumes of the *Boy's Own Paper* had escaped my eye or my affections; *Fighting the Flames* and *The Coral Island* could not fail. But these others went further. A sailor was ill in a cave on a desert island — and a bottle of quinine appeared on the table! Romance and science united. Yet still, one would now and then look at White's *Selborne*, and Chambers's reading-book from English literature. The *Compleat Angler* was borrowed, together with Wisden's Almanack. Old Moore's Almanack, and any other penny directory of information, was always called for in our house. Being sometimes the selected assistant of the organ-tuner — the fee was eightpence — I read histories of the organ, and lamented that our village instrument had not the ingenious eighteenth-century stop which, when pulled out by meddlers, flapped a fox's brush in their faces.

When my tenth year had come, I had discovered the penny dreadful, and over all my reading there spread a veil of *Union Jacks* and *Marvels* and *Magnets*. But still, children must be subject to 'strange fits of passion'; for at the same period the charm of maps and geography, the music of poetry prevailed:

> 'Proud Maisie is in the dell,
>   Walking so early . . .'

> 'O what can ail thee, knight-at-arms,
>   Alone and palely loitering?'

Yet from the first there had been an inclination to those and other less-known perfections, a notion of what the gulf was between Percy's *Reliques* (another riddling title) and the hymn at the open-air service,

> Little streamlet in the dell,
> Who has made you, can you tell?

The song-book even at the infant school had depressed us with,

> Honey-bee, honey-bee, why do you hum?
> I am so happy the summer has come? —

rendered minus the h's. At once,

> Come follow, follow me,
> Ye fairy elves that be,

had established superiority.

Children read with vivid senses things which are, in a sort, their books. The churchyard was a book to us. 'Understandest thou what thou readest?' Well, almost — but the stone-mason is a doubtful authority. Here, it looks as though 'THE ETERNAL COD IS THY REFUGE'. We also pored upon all public notices, on descending hills without properly adjusted skid-pans, on rat and sparrow clubs, on missionary weeks, election promises, and river conservancy. There was *something to read* even on a knife-machine, or the container of Lyle's Golden Syrup.

Having vented all this muddled evidence, I have convinced myself that what children read is a queer story, and I should never, I hope, present Miss or Master with any work in the faith that it would suit. If one could be certain that all hands were washed, the solution would be, perhaps, to leave the young rogues in one's study, and let them find their own giants, and Proud Maisies, and Arks, and Lilliputians. There is one study at any rate, where they would find no work describing them as Tiny Tots. Their self-respect is to be left alone. Nor would they find *Virginibus Puerisque*.

So great is the physical part of childish experience, that books are indeed to them realities. They have their characteristics, to be detested or adored, in their make, feel, and look. The smell of some bindings, the surface of some papers, the tints of some illustrations seem to affect children, especially adversely, even when the contents of the books should have been favourite. Glancing at much contemporary comment on writing, I am inclined to suppose that this kind of practical criticism persists more strongly in years said to be of discretion than has been commonly realized.

(1929)

SUBJECT IN POETRY

'I'm afraid we must keep our hands off his subject-matter,' said an older critic to a younger during a discussion of the poetical wrongdoing of a contemporary, and it seems to be as good a rule as any other for application to all works of art. Our business is rather to consider how a man has expressed what moved him than why the matter moved him; in the time-honoured words, 'it ain't so much the thing 'e sez as the narsty way 'e sez it'. To judge by the world's experience, the chances of a better poem being addressed to a rose than to a policeman are almost overwhelming, and subjects like the moon, the moor, the merry month of May, almost present the poet with a bonus before he starts upon them. But the fact is a challenge to your new poet to be different, to excruciate the bourgeois, to overthrow the odds.

It is not the least agreeable of literary amusements to look through one's poetry books and notice the less usual subjects commemorated there. The few eighteenth-century books accessible here are rich in the most modish and ingenious topics, such as would never have occurred to you and me if we were writing verses. Never — that is, hardly ever; for after all we might have hit upon this title, at necessity's supreme command: 'The Author, Being in Company with Emma, and having no Opportunity of Expressing Certain Doubts he had Conceived of her Sincerity, Conveys to her the following Lines, as a Device to know the Sentiments of her Heart'. (The device was successful. A footnote tells us that Emma returned the paper with her name pencilled against the line: 'Weak my suspicions and unjust my song'.)

It would have been a little harder, for anyone but the predestined singer, to derive a composite inspiration from the following: 'To Mrs. B—— Reading "Julia" with Tears, during a Hard Frost,' or this: 'On a Present to the Author, of Two Impressions from a fine Antique Seal of the Head of Alexander. The one by Lady P——, on Paper; the other by Miss J—— P, in Wax.' The very courteous but alas, very nominal poet offers his genius 'To a Young Lady who objected to Sup with a Party of Both Sexes that Met at a Coffee-House', 'To Laura, on her Receiving a Mysterious Letter from a Methodist Divine', and 'To the Same, on Politics'. Almost all his effusions are as novel, but the titles are as good as the poems that they introduce, perhaps better. It is a little saddening to find an 'Ode on His Grace the Duke of Marlborough converting his Green-house into a Private Theatre' which after all only begins 'Why weeps the Genius of the flowers?'

Sometimes the courage and insight of the older poets are overlooked in our literary histories. Many

critics have done little but ridicule the gifted doctor
who took as his own province in poetical subjects
'The Art of Preserving Health'. Dr. John Armstrong
will nevertheless stand his ground longer than his
careless assailants. It was a bold step, to take the diet,
hygiene, illnesses and remedies of man as the founda-
tions for a spacious house of verse, but the more one
thinks about that, the more one is inclined to agree
with the poet's simple ending:

> the wise of old adored
> One Power of Physic, Melody and Song.

But his success was not equalled by the man who
soon afterwards wrote 'Sickness: in Five Books', nor
can the author of 'The Animalcule: A Tale: occasioned
by his Grace the Duke of Rutland's receiving the
Small-Pox by Inoculation' and 'On the Recovery of a
Lady of Quality from the Small-Pox', compete with
Dr. Armstrong.

The vaccination poet mentioned nevertheless has
his merits if we look into him again, and was himself
the unsurpassed author of a long epistle touching
'Public Spirit in regard to Public Works' — another
theme which might seem dull and prosy but on
reflection glows with deep intellectual fires. There is
nothing meretricious, no false glitter about the poet's
further explanation of his solid title, when he proceeds:
'Of reservoirs, and their use; of draining fens, and
building bridges, cutting canals and repairing har-

bours, and stopping inundations, making rivers navigable, building lighthouses; of agriculture, gardening,
and planting for the noblest uses; of commerce; of
public roads; of public buildings, viz. squares, streets,
mansions, palaces, courts of justice, senate-houses,
theatres, hospitals, churches, colleges, the variety of
worthies produced by the letter, of colonies. The slave-
trade censured, etc.' The resulting work was offered
to the Prince of Wales in 1737, and has a renewed
interest at this moment, when the public is so critical
of its great cities in their details.

Even great and familiar poets may surprise us with
the oddity of some of their titles. Coleridge, who
went his own way through everything, could publish
a little piece called 'To a Lady offended by a Sportive
Observation that Women have no Souls', and another,
'Inscription for a Seat by the Road Side Half-Way Up
a Steep Hill Facing South'; and this although he had
in earlier days met with a good deal of loud laughter
for his all too affectionate and brotherly address 'To
a Young Ass; Its Mother being Tethered near It'.
Shelley, likewise pioneer and visionary, sometimes
had his off days, especially in his early period, when
he wrote the 'Sonnet on Launching Some Bottles
Filled with Knowledge into the Bristol Channel'.
Keats was responsible for three sonnets as follows:
'To a Young Lady who Sent Me a Laurel Crown',
'On Receiving a Laurel Crown from Leigh Hunt',
and 'To the Ladies who Saw me Crown'd"; and

unfortunately these do not indicate any suspicion or recognition on the poet's part that the performance had a humorous side. The subjects of Tennyson, chosen with regard to due originality, and at the same time to official dignity, might be expected to avoid any obvious 'queerness', yet there is something a little too laconic in the title 'Happy; the Leper's Bride', and when he proudly announces 'God and The Universe', only to settle the point in half a dozen harmless lines, one feels that it was no more than a Chinese attack.

Turning to some modern masters, we continue to come upon the usual subject and the peculiar title. Mr. Thomas Hardy, who was writing poems since about 1860 until the other day, was no eccentric; but his long campaign was seldom fought out with the ordinary aims or resources. The irony which so often sent its quick current through his poems often lurks in the titles also, and the 'unconscious humour' of some poets already mentioned will not so easily be ascribed to him. He is unmistakable even in the brief compass of title. 'At a Seaside Town in 1869 (Young Lover's Reverie)', 'The Memorial Brass: 186—', 'Honeymoon Time at an Inn' — could we ascribe these and the hundreds of similar labels to any other hand? No, nor that awkward looking one, 'Mismet'.

Dr. Bridges generally found himself indebted for his poems to the classical sort of themes and situations; his friend G. M. Hopkins, whose remarkable and

inimitable poems he finely edited in 1918, is no conventional poet in his style or his starting-points
either, as may soon be shown 'The Handsome
Heart, at a gracious Answer', 'Pied Beauty', 'That
Nature is a Heraclitean Fire and of the comfort of the
Resurrection' are examples of his medieval-seeing
subjects.

Nowadays, it may often be doubted whether the
title of a poem is really equivalent to its subject.
Usually in the past there has been no uncertainty
about it, the poet who told us he was writing 'Thoughts
Occasioned by the Death of a Favourite Domestic, of
a Quartan Fever, on Christmas Day 1783' really was
writing about that unhappy event. To-day the
tendency is to inscribe a legend like 'Mene Mene
Tekel Upharsin' over some casual descriptive notes on
one's depression in a Bucharest hotel, or to throw
out some blunt word like 'Corpse' as a preliminary to
reflections on a rural scene. Ophelia heard there
were tricks in the world, and nowadays she could have
substantiated that in looking through her supplies of
new verse. To begin with 'The Feather Bed', and
quickly be floundering among the billows of dementia
praecox, and clawing at the crags of sheer nonsense —
rocks which do not by custom turn to beds of down;
to be told to get ready for 'Village', and then to find
out that the parson's gardener and the doctor's
chauffeur are fiends incarnate, the respected brewer's
traveller and the schoolmaster have most streaked and

spotted souls, the milkmaid did away with her grey father for his insurance money — all these developments would meet Ophelia without warning in our period of unlimited subject-matter in poetry. She might prefer to go back for a little fresh air to the days when a poet put down the words 'A Daisy' and began: 'The daisy is a happy flower'. But to everything its season, except, I submit, the occasional affixing of the conclusive word 'Poem' to some new but not nice derangement of epitaphs.

(1926)

GEOGRAPHICAL IMPROVEMENTS

THE process of modernization has reached, they say, the very geography which the rising generation studies. It is not so long ago that most of us looked on the subject with a certain disfavour, and indeed considered it as milk for babies, not to be throned aloft with the strong man's pabulum, his Greek dramatists, his calculus. We agreed to disregard the round world, having suffered much at an earlier stage because of it, and our recollection of what Nova Zembla was famous for, and where the principal volcanoes flourished, and which rivers were navigable between Rio Janeiro and Bahia Blanca were allowed to subside. And now — they have changed all that. Geography has become, according to report, a subject at once fascinating and socially possible. Exactly how, is beyond us pre-geographic people; it is sufficient to report the accomplished fact. Rumour says, moreover, that the age of 'insolent Greece and haughty Rome' is scholastically wearing out: that nowadays a certain disfavour applies to the elegant conduct of Ciceronian rhetoric. 'Quid dicam, hac iuventute?' What is the Globe coming to?

It would surprise me, nevertheless, if the modern geographical apparatus is more agreeable and inspiring than some of the discarded text-books of the past.

The eighteenth-century schoolboy may not have recognized 'Mr. Salmon's Geography' as a curious, romantic treasury, but it is now as good a shillings-worth as the old bookstalls offer — the section on the Hottentots alone is worth the money. Other works of the kind are to be had; but perhaps the most accept-able relics of a world as yet unanatomized by scientific accuracy and undiminished by Marconi are the atlases, maps and plans in which many collectors and dealers find a lifetime of fond labour. In the kingdom of Geography the province of Cartography is certainly rich in attractions, and so long as we are not obliged to reach a destination we may well prefer the maps of a century ago, or more.

Here is an early edition of *Gulliver's Travels* with a number of maps drawn in the ancient style, well worthy of a glance now and then, although we can-not follow Gulliver in all his peregrinations. How stately and fine is the engraving, whether of moun-tainous islands or embayed coasts, with their names, or of the adventurous barques in mid-ocean, and the challenging but official whales wielding their tails like dogs, and spouting with enthusiasm! One of these plates includes, as well as one tall ship and a couple of sea-beasts, a portion reserved for 'Japan'. To the north lies a blank space styled 'Parts Unknown'. Then, south of these gaunt wastes, we see a large slab labelled 'Land of Iesso' — not a bad rendering of Yezo, seeing that it was about 200 years ago. South again, below the 'Sea of Cornea' lies 'Japan'. It is the same, but not the same, here are 'Osacca', 'Meaco', 'Iedo', but also 'Toy Pt.' and 'Red Pt.' and 'Ongeluckig I.' Whether the author of *Gulliver* cared much for these peculiarities, or believed in the map, is doubtful. It was he who wrote elsewhere:

> Geographers in Afric Maps
> With Savage Pictures fill their Gaps;
> And o'er unhabitable Downs
> Place Elephants for want of Towns.

A great collection of maps of this class is to be examined in the principal booksellers' shops, and occasionally one finds examples in the miscellaneous 'cheap lots' of the stallkeeper. The well-known London authority on prints and books, Mr. Francis Edwards, has lately sent out a catalogue called 'Old Time Cartography', full of picturesque glimpses. Old Ortelius's atlas, issued at Amsterdam in 1603, is described as adorned with galleons, neptunes, mermaids, sea monsters, Jonah, the Grand Cham, camels, etc. Jonah was a genuine inspiration, and Ortelius evidently a strict Fundamentalist. His map of China is embellished with ships, crucifixion, wind car, etc. Many of the European maps are fringed with coats of arms, and sweet little cherubs sit up aloft to look after them. These old and soothing relics are by no means out of the ordinary man's reach, but occasionally a special rarity occurs. Mr. Edwards

R   257

catalogues one such — an atlas published by Moses Pitt at Oxford in 1681. It costs £150, and must be a lordly piece of work; on large paper, with 89 double-page maps in colours and gold, gold lettering and ornamentation through the text, too, a binding of morocco, glowing red, with golden trelliswork about it. Why all this labour and luxury over an atlas? The answer is, it was the dedication copy, and belonged to King Charles II. Did he look at it? The answer is, Not so often as he looked at Nell Gwyn.

The country maps issued in out-of-the-way towns in England frequently included engravings of the most popular local antiquities, which make them most agreeable. It is this happy superfluity, this willingness on the part of the craftsman to do a little more than the necessity, which gives old-fashioned things their distinction. The old school were not disposed to be called 'unprofitable servants'. And so, a map was no doubt just serviceable by itself as with little inset pictures of the market-place or the priory — but the publisher threw them in out of love. And in our harder times, we love him for it. Sweet be his rest below the old tower which in this corner of his sixpenny survey rises clear above the cleanly street and rattling coach of 1830!

These thoughts do not inhibit one's admiration of modern maps, ordinance surveys and the like. The advance that man has been making in science at large has not been withheld from the map-maker. Napoleon himself must have marvelled had he seen what excellent maps, in what beautiful styles of printing and colouring, were placed at the service of every subaltern in the last war. The rate at which edition succeeded edition, even if it frequently lagged behind the rate of local alterations, and marked in solid black the phantasmal tatters of blown-out streets, was a constant wonder. The system of 'conventional sign' for quarries, churches, windmills, bridges, and the varieties of type in which the names of places were set, made map-reading a fairly simple thing. It is amusing and instructive to compare a modern trench map with an ancient one (and the repeated wars in Flanders make it possible to view the very same piece of ground through widely different mediums). The best of our modern intelligence officers might be reduced to frowns and knottings of the Shakespearean brow by a 1745 plan of Lille. The old style of fortification appears on the map somehow as a highly complicated starfish or elaborate optical illusion. One wants the assistance of my Uncle Toby.

In most parishes of England, the vicar or rector has a tithe-map, or knows where it is kept. The geography of one's own village can be fascinating with such a map to provide a check on failing memory or human error. Merely to acquire all the names of buildings, fields, turnings, paths, mounds in sight of one's house is a sufficient recreation, and depends on luck as well as judgment; for the old ploughman or horse-keeper who

knows every bush and stile is not always in a reminis-
cent mood, and is easily filled with suspicion as to
'what 'e might be after'. Place-names are in this
century systematically registered and interpreted,
with rich results; for almost as remarkable as what
disappears from the earth is what hangs on century
after century. The mild joke by the terms of which A
remarks: 'My people came over with the Conqueror'
and B answers: 'Yes, and found mine here', is often
paralleled by the surviving place-names of an English
village.

Passing by such oddities as maps done in needlework
or carved out on hunting-horns, or tattooed on ancient
mariners, one might spend a moment or two among
certain literary ones. There is that troublesome one in
Shakespeare's *King Lear*.

'Give me the map there. Know we have divided
In three our kingdom.'

There is Charles Lamb's shadow 'South-Sea House'
with its 'huge charts, which subsequent discoveries
have antiquated; duty maps of Mexico, dim as dreams
— and soundings of the Bay of Panama'. Leigh Hunt's
essay on 'The World of Books', takes a different path.
He suggests the preparation of 'a very curious map,
in which this world of books might be delineated and
filled up'; in which 'a circle of stars would tell us where
Galileo lived', and 'the Stormy spirit of the Cape,
stationed there for ever by Camoens', would loom

like a mountain. Nothing done yet, though some have tried to make a literary atlas, in any point equals the eager fancy of hearty Leigh Hunt.

Among geographers proper, Lamb and Hunt would commend us to see that the name of Michael Drayton is held in remembrance. This old poet, fabled to have been one of Shakespeare's tavern companions, wrote his geography of Great Britain in verse, to the extent of thirty books. If it is any sign of grace to have read all these, the present writer is qualified; but from the publication of Drayton's *Polyolbion* more than three hundred years ago until now most people have preferred their geography in prose. Drayton, aware of this insubordination, prefixed a preface to the second part, saying 'I have met with barbarous ignorance and base detraction; such a cloud hath the Devil drawn over the world's judgment'; the booksellers were attacked for their preference for 'beastly and abominable trash'. There is something familiar in these observations. But Drayton is not the worse geographer on that account, and if the present enthusiasm lasts we may see him issued by the Ordnance Survey as a companion to their temptations, sheet upon sheet, into the country places.

(1926)

SIEGFRIED SASSOON'S
POETRY

THE prevailing trouble of poetic characters appears to be an inability to vary from the strict business of inspiration, or what is presumed to be pure poetry. Shadwell, we know, never deviated into sense; but there are those machine-like singers who never deviate into nonsense. 'Verse, a breeze 'mid blossoms straying' has latterly erected for itself wire fences and warnings against trespass. The pretence of emancipation has actually been part of the process of enclosure. 'I am now going to create new forms,' says the modern poet, 'I shall be very busy for some time. High is our calling. I have the call. I have no leisure to pursue anything except the essential, which I am bound to reveal.' From such notions it arises that much new verse is monotonous, unsubstantial, and irrelevant; it does not comfort, but burn; it does not burn with ardour, but with coldness. One is reminded of the proverbial blind man's hunt in a dark room for a needle which is not there.

If the brevity and agreeable imperfection of life argue against any over-estimate of serious activities, even the writing of poetry, and demand a full use of the passions and characteristics, they do not exonerate the artist from perfecting his method and his equipment. The theorist who, stern as the lady missionary of Chinese cartoons, stalks on towards his Holy Grail in a rarefied stylistic atmosphere, does not always succeed in avoiding the ditch. His bluer blues and flatter flats are not habitually so accomplished as they might be. Rhythm and verbal suggestion are old mysteries, and do not yield themselves instantly to the most select determination of neophytes. Intensity of insight even is not sure to produce a poem likely to live unless the writer experiencing it has grown into a certainty of poetic style, a certainty implying not one sole avenue of verse, but a system of routes capable of many possibilities, and branches. The charities, the aspirations, the illusions, the situations of our general humanity are now, as ever, the grand influences to which a poet must be unstrainedly responsive; yet all those may not awaken a compelling clearness and freshness of poetry in him without a comparable openness of feeling in the region of language and presentation.

Of those distinguished writers who have displayed, retained, enlarged an openness of judgment in new poetry, and who have made discoveries for themselves without the onset of hallucinations menacing all that had been previously regarded, Siegfried Sassoon is the brightest example. At the moment, perhaps, it is necessary to insist that Mr. Sassoon, the author of a prose work acclaimed everywhere, is first and foremost a poet. The *Memoirs of a Fox-Hunting Man*, that endlessly intuitive and gleaming retrospect, is not only a prose masterpiece; it is the proof, the double-sure assurance of the qualifications of Mr. Sassoon as poet. It has pleased two races of men — those who did not catch its subtler beckonings, and those who did. 'Cultivate simplicity, Coleridge.' Mr. Sassoon has acted on that far-reaching advice — simplicity is the mother of variety. We stand on our side of the corner, and if we remain friends with simplicity we have a feeling for the blind side. What poetry may be in a full definition I am not sure; but I believe that it includes a special instinct for the other sides of the corners of circumstance. There are no dead shadows, empty silences, blank unchartable continents for a faculty of intellectual and spiritual affection such as that which is found in Mr. Sassoon.

There is, in the volume called *The Heart's Journey*, a brief but extremely fruitful poem in which Mr. Sassoon gives his own picture of the sympathies involved in the poetic sympathy, the sources of the various curiosity supplying the imaginative experience:

> In me, past, present, future meet
> To hold long chiding conference.
> My lusts usurp the present tense
> And strangle Reason in his seat.
> My loves leap through the future's fence
> To dance with dream-enfranchised feet.

In me the cave-man clasps the seer,
And garlanded Apollo goes
Chanting to Abraham's deaf ear.
In me the tiger sniffs the rose.
    Look in my heart, kind friends, and tremble,
    Since there your elements assemble.

These are not all the elements which in concentration
or in single recurrence produce the groundwork of
Mr. Sassoon's poetry, and command for it that
abundance of interest and ease of transition from one
sphere to another which we seek in vain through so
much neological verse. But these seem like the chief-
tains of his 'force of all arms'. It is his good fortune
always to understand that man cannot wholly understand, to accept the ins and outs of the prodigious
current of evolution, and to possess accordingly an
impulsive and humorous freedom.

This statement may be voted incorrect by some
readers who, as most of us did, first met the poems of
Mr. Sassoon during the European War. Few volumes
of our time have been the subject of more animated
discussion than the widely read *Counter-Attack*. Now
that we are able to review our war again without
terrible dreams and distorting projections of formerly
unsuspected prejudice, it may be hoped that *Counter-
Attack* will find out many readers still. It does not
offer, or pretend to offer, what is ridiculously advertised as 'all the war', neither does it make all other

war books unnecessary. But for certain times and seasons and figures and forces of battle, Mr. Sassoon was and is the unsurpassed spokesman. Deferring this theme for a moment, let us revert to the question how far *Counter-Attack* contradicts the observation that humour is one of Mr. Sassoon's inalienable angels.

Then, let us revert to 1917 and 1918; to a feverish, tired, bloodstained, brainsick world; to those frenzied shrieks to heaven, and more dangerous silences. It is difficult now. Even in peace there are individual battlefields and defeats which have no compensating adventure, no classic touch. But by 1917 the adventure and the classic touch were considerably worn out in the man-eating clay of the Somme, and the fatherless parlours of 'Corons de maisons', and Love Lane, and Markstrasse. There were many hundred thousand men in France and Flanders alone who had emerged from attack into attack, and then into the next attack, well aware that they must become one morning mere heaps in oozing shell-holes, or bundles on the barbed wire. And still most of these men, obedient, unassuming, mute as Spartans, were expected to smile:

> Are we down-hearted?
> NO————.
> Think we shall win?

No answer. But beyond these, in their unimaginable imprisonment, there were those hysterical cries and that savage silence devoted to a very much unknown God labelled Victory. In these Satanically laughable conditions of human misunderstanding (and here I write from a particular hatred of the period and the agonies of the Passchendaele illusion), a poet was found with the strength of mind to sacrifice everything, even the traditions of poetry, even his earlier artistic plan, in order that he might make audible and intelligible in England and elsewhere the weeping Truth:

> He went and said it very clear,
> He went and shouted it in their ear.

Such emphasis was essential. *Counter-Attack* was what its double-barrelled title said it was. It was a gun let off at the universal enemy with grim jokes chalked on some of the shells — but the time did not admit of many such jokes. It was an individual's endeavour, under a conviction that things were going from bad to worse, to pull the line of civilization together.

In order to carry out this step towards reformation, several kinds of warlike stories, several tactical ideas were needed. Most important of all was the provision of a Natural History of the War:

> a monster of such frightful mien
> As, to be hated, needs but to be seen;

and, for that point, a profusion of absurdity was already circulated everywhere, even in the trenches.

We smile at medieval bestiaries, at man-serpents and mountain-whales; but between 1914 and 1917 there had been some popular errors about the face and appetites of War, just as chimerical. Then came Mr. Sassoon. He ejected the chimera:

> The place was rotten with dead; green clumsy legs
> High-booted, sprawled and grovelled along the saps;
> And trunks, face downward, in the sucking mud,
> Wallowed like trodden sand-bags loosely filled;
> And naked sodden buttocks, mats of hair,
> Bulged, clotted heads slept in the plastering slime.
> And then the rain began — the jolly old rain!
>
> A yawning soldier knelt against the bank,
> Staring across the morning blear with fog;
> He wondered when the Allemands would get busy;
> And then, of course, they started with five-nines
> Traversing, sure as fate, and never a dud.
> Mute in the clamour of shells he watched them burst
> Spouting dark earth and wire with gusts from hell,
> While posturing giants dissolved in drifts of smoke.

In such passages, the usual surprising power of the imaginative temperament is exceeded. It is, as one looks back, bewildering that a human being should retain such sensibility in that burning fiery furnace.

Besides presenting the portrait of War, the poet of *Counter-Attack* gave us something which at that time was becoming almost as strange — the recollected charm of Peace. In this subject Mr. Sassoon had shown his understanding and his typical union of familiar and unfamiliar matters, realistic and fanciful, on several occasions. The first sonnet in a quarto volume privately printed for him twenty years ago — what a Young Poet he was, and is! — would alone entitle him to remembrance among those many Englishmen who have answered the 'nods and becks' of thrilling tranquillity with an added pleasantness. It is such a beautiful, natural song of personality and England's meaning that I shall include it here:

Come in this hour to set my spirit free
When earth is no more mine though night goes out,
And stretching forth these arms I cannot be
Lord of winged sunrise and dim Arcady;
When fieldward boys far off with clack and shout
Still scare the birds away in sudden rout
Come ere my heart grows old, and filled with doubt.
In passional summer dawns I call for thee.

When the first lark goes up to look for day,
And morning glimmers out of dreams, come then,
A shadow amid shadows; over grey
Wide misty wealds to bring me on my way:
For I am lone, a dweller among men,
Hunger'd for what my heart shall never say.

It was not merely the mystical intimacies of solitude that Mr. Sassoon made poetic. He saw other glories, which are mostly accepted without honour; and by the time that he was writing *The Old Huntsman* (a book which should be reprinted as it stood first) and *Counter-Attack*, he called up these equally with the more visionary. Still it was

> Come down from heaven to meet me;

still he invoked the inheritances of

> all the beauty that has been,
> And stillness from the pools of Paradise.

But he made us perceive the values of old and then savagely annihilated commonplaces; his range of feeling created such truthful, humorous, pathetic reminders as the well-known *Dreamers*, namely you and me:

> I see them in foul dug-outs, gnawed by rats,
>   And in the ruined trenches, lashed with rain,
> Dreaming of things they did with balls and bats,
>   And mocked by hopeless longing to regain
> Bank-holidays, and picture shows, and spats,
>   And going to the office in the train.

Sometimes the pity of war, the pastoral dream, the joke between friends, the smiling philosophy were harmonized into one Sassoonian comment, as in *The Investiture*:

God with a Roll of Honour in His hand
Sits welcoming the heroes who have died,
While sorrowless angels ranked on either side
Stand easy in Elysium's meadow-land.
Then *you* come shyly through the garden gate,
Wearing a blood-soaked bandage on your head;
And God says something kind because you're dead,
And homesick, discontented with your fate . . .

Without a strong and subtle humour this sort of poem, and all its changes of note and colour, could never have been written.

But the urgency of the world's misery called for another tone, besides these; and *Counter-Attack* employed a type of sarcastic verse which Mr. Sassoon developed for the particular case. He struck out with mockery of the apathy, or false ardours, of the period:

Does it matter? – losing your legs? . . .

He made poetry talk over the telephone, 'to any dead officer':

Our Politicians swear
They won't give in till Prussian Rule's been trod
Under the Heel of England. . . . Are you there?
Yes . . . and the War won't end for at least two years;
But we've got stacks of men . . . I'm blind with tears,
Staring into the dark. Cheero!
I wish they'd killed you in a decent show.

271

Nothing is more certain than that Mr. Sassoon himself realized the difference, in the way of essential
poetry, between these searing colloquial verses of
desperation and the full-toned lyrics, the delicately
profound descriptions and interpretations which his
nature could and should be comprised in. But then,
as ever in less precipitous style, he refused to regard
'pure poetry' as the sole business of a poet. Mr.
Sassoon, standing with admirable reverence before
the mysteries which sometimes vouchsafe us the inevitable achievement, may be seen with his notebook
ready for the prosaically amusing or detached detail.
It does not concern him whether what he writes can
all pass the tricky turnstiles of higher criticism into the
pantheon of the selected sublime and absolute intense.

Among the subordinate verse-moods of Mr. Sassoon
('let the music of them be recreational'), I have always
found an invincible happiness in the conversation
poems, which are agreeably represented as the ex-
pressions of a slightly awkward individual not quite
sure whether he is trespassing, but amiably observing
as much as the authorities permit. I like Mr. Sassoon
with his notebook better than the austere finalists with
the most recent psychological manuals. He has a
knack of discovering places on earth and in heaven
which they miss, as he 'arrives obscurely pondering
on the past, Sententious thus. . . .' When, in 1926,
Mr. Sassoon put forth a collection of his whims and
oddities, it met with less likeable caprices on the part

of reviewers, who assailed him for not succeeding as a
satirist. Yet his book was not called, nor could it be,
a volume of satires. His title was *Satirical Poems*.
Flogging the town, in the style of Juvenal or Charles
Churchill, demands a degree of ferocity and a self-
certainty which he would not claim. His sense is
rather, even in his indignation, 'There, but for the
grace of God . . .' He is anxious to make all allow-
ances, and look the other way at least the first occasion:

> Fountains upheave pale plumes against the sky,
> Murmuring, 'Their Majesties came sauntering by —
> Was it but yesterday?' . . . Proud fountains sigh
> Toward the long glades in golden foliage clad,
> 'Kurfursts could do no wrong.' . . . And the woods
>   reply,
> 'Take them for what they were, they weren't so bad.'

While he walks in his quietly expectant and cheerfully inquiring easiness about the nooks and corners
of civilization, Mr. Sassoon receives very vividly the
impression of event, character, environment and
changefulness. He perceives atmosphere revealing
itself in images, in living personations of the past, the
present, and time to come. He often tells us his
story with a beguiling ambiguity, an inimitable private
gesture which explains that he is sure he is only
guessing, and is happy in his pastime. He whistles
while he sets up his colonnades and invents his masks
of history:

s   273

'*Of course you saw the Villa d'Este Gardens,*'
Writes one of my Italianistic friends.
Of course; of course; I saw them in October,
Spired with pinaceous ornamental gloom
Of that arboreal elegy the cypress.

Those fountains, too, 'like ghosts of cypresses' —
(The phrase occurred to me while I was leaning
On an old balustrade; imbibing sunset;
Wrapped in my verse vocation) — how they linked
    me
With Byron, Landor, Liszt, and Robert Brown-
    ing! . . .
A *Liebestraum* of Liszt cajoled my senses.
My language favoured Landor, chaste and formal.
My intellect (though slightly in abeyance)
Functioned against a Byronistic background.
Then Browning jogged my elbow; bade me hob-nob
With some forgotten painter of dim frescoes
That haunt the Villa's intramural twilight.

While roaming in the Villa d'Este Gardens
I felt like that . . . and fumbled for my note-book.

If the universe is planned by the Deity sometimes de-
picted in Mr. Sassoon's filial verse, then the elder
poets look on their successors with regard and hope;
and it would be perhaps Coleridge, and Landor, and
Edward Fitzgerald who are 'watching with no small

interest' the resourceful though unpretentious 'satirical poems' of Mr. Sassoon.

Under that nonchalance of bearing, magnificence of mind is found. We deplore the barrenness of the imaginative faculty in our time, the absence of the seer and the watch-tower; but in Mr. Sassoon's work there are passages on the grand scale. Such is the Greek-drama beginning of the prelude to *Counter-Attack*, withdrawing the veil of night and of ignorance from the line of battle:

> Dim, gradual thinning of the shapeless gloom
> Shudders to drizzling daybreak that reveals
> Disconsolate men who stamp their sodden boots
> And turn dulled, sunken faces to the sky
> Haggard and hopeless.

Such, again, is the marshalling and march-past of old actions in the autumn afternoon at Blenheim Palace:

> In wars which burst before the South Sea Bubble
> Muskets explode, hussars and pike-men plunder,
> While Churchill, stimulating martial trouble,
> Perturbs Palatinates with smoke and thunder. . . .

More spacious still is the last of the *Satirical Poems*, the reanimation of the legend of Apollo and Daphne under the images of 'Solar Eclipse'. It contains at once the supposed event, the enthusiasm of ancient and lost minds, and the colours thrown on later ages from that mythology:

275

Daphne turns
At the wood edge in bronze and olive gloom:
Sickness assails the sun, whose blazing disc
Dwindles: the Eden of those auburn slopes
Lours in the tarnished copper of eclipse.

Yet virgin, in her god-impelled approach
To Graeco-Roman ravishment, she waits
While the unsated python slides to crush
Her lust-eluding fleetness. Envious Jove
Rumbles Olympus. All the classic world
Leans breathless toward the legend she creates.
From thunderous vapour smites the immortal
    beam. . . .
Then, crowned with fangs of foliage, flames the god.

In earlier days, Mr. Sassoon found his poems in the observation of country life more frequently than he appears to do now. Indeed, one of the sonnets in *The Heart's Journey* is a farewell to the delight he once had in natural influences and contacts:

Alone, I hear the wind about my walls. . . .
Wind of the city night, south-west and warm —
Rain-burdened wind, your homely sound recalls
Youth; and a distant country-side takes form,
Comforting with memory-sight my town-taxed
    brain. . . .
Wind from familiar fields and star-tossed trees,
You send me walking lonely through dark and rain
Before I'd lost my earliest ecstacies. . . .

It is not unlikely that this farewell is only for a time; strange, should that fountain which has played in many melodies and freshening dispensations through all Mr. Sassoon's verse hitherto, fail to rise in his spirit now. If this were to happen, the Nature-pages already secure in his work would be already considerable enough. No more delicate sense than his is found in contemporary verse for the simple thanksgiving to some wise Wonder implicit in beautiful description. The art of honour in poetry is against 'long prayers'; it dwells in attentiveness of body and soul, in the devoted and matured recording of the way in which Nature moves:

> Out in the night there's autumn-smelling gloom
> Crowded with whispering trees; across the park
> A hollow cry of hounds like lonely bells:
> And I know that the clouds are moving across the
>   moon;
> The low, red, rising moon. Now herons call
> And wrangle by their pool; and hooting owls
> Sail from the wood above pale stooks of oats.

Mr. Sassoon is a poet able to be judged either by complete compositions or by short fragments, single lines, in which his fantasy and imagination unite; his renderings of Nature shine in the briefest quotation:

The old horse lifts his face and thanks the light. . . .

Tossed on the glittering air they soar and skim,
Whose voices make the emptiness of light
A windy palace. . . .

Voices heard through veils and faces blind
To the kind light of my autumnal gleanings.

Withdrawing from the external and physical aspects
of things for a time, Mr. Sassoon has latterly been
allured to poems chiefly lyrical by a mystical simplicity underlying the spectacle of activity and power.
The Heart's Journey represents this calm sequestered
phase of his poetical work. By its contents the reader
may readily discover that Mr. Sassoon travels, according to the chances of experience and temperament,
autour de sa chambre; the scene is no more lavish, for the
greater part of the book, than 'a midnight interior',
but the poet's walls vanish into the wide expanses of
intuition on the given word of a secret messenger. Nor
is the word laden with fear or discord. The original
confidence of Mr. Sassoon in the nature of things has
returned in a new light; the early world of flowers has
been transformed into something akin to Vaughan's
benediction, 'Heaven's Lily and the earth's chaste
Rose.' The likeness of his idea to that of Vaughan,
and his desire that it might become more and
more radiant in him, animated his perfect sonnet at

Vaughan's grave. But Mr. Sassoon's private hymns and utterances of the undying brightness have their own unborrowed qualities:

Let there be life, said God. And what He wrought
Went past in myriad marching lives, and brought
This hour, this quiet room, and my small thought
Holding invisible vastness in its hands.

Let there be God, say I. And what I've done
Goes onward like the splendour of the sun
And rises up in rapture and is one
With the white power of conscience that commands.

Let Life be God. . . . What wail of fiend or wraith
Dare mock my glorious angel where he stands
To fill my dark with fire, my heart with faith?

The sense of the infinite does indeed, for the writer of those lines, 'roll through all things'. Even his most reserved and haunted hour is busy with the sound of the mortal drama. He speaks of his revelation with a warmth of gratitude, and the listener is aware not of some distant marvel but of the ticking clock, the 'patient lamp', the rumour of late traffic, and a deep devotion suddenly filling all the place. Few of us are spiritually rich enough to refuse this generous piety,

> granting strength to find
> From lamp and flower simplicity of mind.

Apart from his poems in conversational style, Mr. Sassoon has the faculty of making his work lyrical. His sonnets are songs, his epigrams even have their music. His best known piece is that cry of release in 1919:

Everyone suddenly burst out singing;
And I was filled with such delight
As prisoned birds must find in freedom
Winging wildly across the white
Orchards and dark green fields; on; on; and out of
sight.

Occasionally he, like all the poets in less anxious times, allows verses to take shape for their sound rather than their significance. He is one of the disciplinarians of words, but he now and then gives a holiday and lets them combine in some pleasant dance 'for music':

Whence you came I cannot tell;
Only — with your joy you start
Chime on chime from bell on bell
In the cloisters of my heart.

There, to be sure, no ambitious meaning is intended. As Shenstone, that brilliant amateur of critical observation, said long ago, a certain flimsiness is necessary to a song. The melody is the thing, and Mr Sassoon calls up the despised 'sentimental' adjective and the rejected idyllic convention with enthusiasm if they appear best for his cadences. His catholicity of values does not fail to characterize the expression, as well as the occasion, of his verse. He will not lightly dismiss any established term or form.

The preparedness of the verbal and metrical artist, which was named above as an unalterable condition of fresh poetical achievements, always has been part of his powers. He can never have fallen into the attractive error of fancying his chance without mastering the principles. The peculiar assurance which in poetics as in war leads into bottomless pits — 'It'll all be all right on the night' — never left him floundering. Prior to the access of his poetical concentrations, due method of language, of rhythm and rhyme or its related groups of sound awaited his discovery of new worlds to conquer. He has not forgotten the old jingle of the writing-master, easily transferable to the calligraphy of poetry:

> Take great care,
> And you'll write fair;

not that he finally appears as a somewhat frightened and suppressed compiler of correct phrase and measure. He calls us on with a beautiful quickness, he sustains us with a deeper consonance — the preservation of old ways which are still excellent for their purpose, blending with the innovation required by new turns of feeling, opinion and incident.

In illustration of this fineness in Mr. Sassoon's art of poetry, one or two matters easily suggest them-

selves. First, he has made an especial friend of the
alexandrine, the 'needless alexandrine' which has
generally been driven away from the doors of English
verse without a hope. As it suits our living speech,
Mr. Sassoon has readily brought it into respectability.
It drags no wounded length along as it impresses its
trust on us:

'Pass it along, the wiring party's going out' —
And yawning sentries mumble, 'Wirers going out.'
Unravelling; twisting; hammering stakes with
    muffled thud,
They toil with stealthy haste and anger in their
    blood.

And again, with increased accomplishment in tones
and variations:

We forget our fear. . . .
And, while the uncouth Even begins to lour less
    near,
Discern the mad magnificence whose storm-light
    throws
Wild shadows on these after-thoughts that send your
    brain
Back beyond Peace, exploring sunken ruinous
    roads.
Your brain, with files of flitting forms hump-backed
    with loads,
On its own helmet hears the tinkling drops of rain, —

Follows to an end some night-relief, and strangely
   sees
The quiet no-man's-land of daybreak, jagg'd with
   trees
That loom like giant Germans . . .
                I'll go with you, then. . . .

Another of his revitalizing technical capacities concerns vocabulary. When he is in his mood of satirical perception, he is inventive of a remarkable series of new worlds, in which he unerringly coadunates (the manner is infectious!) the sublime and the ridiculous. Moreover, in order to banter us still more amusingly and fantastically, he often causes these to run an obstacle-race of extraordinary rhyming. *Satirical Poems* is one long masterpiece of this dexterous wit of form, this parody of intellectual tabulation:

Putting aside enigmas of technique, —
In calm cynosural canvases I seek
Some psycho-coefficient unconfessed . . .
A glum (though lingually-exempted) guest,
I analyse the output; which includes
Complacent persons opulently poised
In unawareness that their names are noised
In highbrow cliques as 'psychologic nudes'.

Putting aside the other enigmas of discriminating the merits of Mr. Sassoon's verse in critical jargon, I may sum up my view very briefly. We have in him a poet of considerable productiveness, but no way inclined to scuffle for novelty or occasion; he writes as he is impelled. His impulses are abundant, for they come from an eagerness in daily contact, in deeper contemplation, in thoughts that are borne from beyond the horizon. His expression is vivid, for he believes in the life rather than the death of man's patiently enlarged means of communication; he has a gift of music, the charm which overrules the rest in poetry. Mr. Sassoon is, and has long been, an English poet answering the demands of tradition and leading the way for the progressive sensibility. It may not be the least valuable thing to note that his work is as *readable* as it is copious; and, if it failed in reflection of the unseen, it would still be fertile in its pictures and estimates of ourselves. But it does not fail in its heavenward correspondences. It is lit with promises and beamings of sunrise beyond chronology.

(1928)